A rich resource at a critical time [illegible] e fine line between praxis and the[illegible] a relevant whole. It is obvious that Das and Hamoud approach this conversation with experience, and because of that, they are able to move the conversation beyond simple platitudes, compassionate emotions and biblical proof texting. This is a theological treatise that needs to be read no matter where you stand in the socio-political positioning of the day. More importantly it is a book that places demands on you if you are truly going to follow Jesus.

Gary V. Nelson, PhD
President, Tyndale University College & Seminary,
Toronto, Ontario, Canada

Forced displacement and homelessness is a physical reality for a growing number of humans and a spiritual reality for us all. When God pulled out all stops to show his solution, he didn't write a book but was himself displaced, becoming flesh, running towards us, stretching wide his arms. The teachings of this book fly in the face of current fear-driven conclusions about migration and immigration. However, Das and Hamoud don't ultimately write to change our minds or politics (though I'll be absorbing and sharing its truths). It is written so more of us will follow Jesus Christ in fleshing out the heart of God for our world's refugees. And, miracles of miracles, as we run towards the displaced and homeless we (and many of them) find the Displaced Deity, making his home in us. As he promised . . . Anyone who loves me will obey my teaching. My Father will love them, and we will come to them and make our home with them (John 14:23).

Paul Carline
Director, Inter-Cultural Ministries,
Canadian Baptists of Atlantic Canada

Rupen Das and Brent Hamoud, two highly qualified scholars with big hearts for ministry, especially serving vulnerable individuals, have provided this valuable resource for theological students and faculty in the twenty-first century. When you read this book, you are offered a comprehensive initiation to a ministry to the displaced.

We hope that we shall soon live in a world where no one is ever forced to flee their homes, villages, towns, and country . . . Alas! We seem to be far from this ideal situation. Until the dream comes true, anyone who has a heart and feels compelled to dedicate time to ministry among refugees, migrants and stateless people, now has available to them a carefully crafted guide. The reader is provided with rich information about "Strangers in the Kingdom," historical landmarks, human-rights tools, with theological and missiological foundations.

Equally important is the series of case studies with which the authors engage the readers in the second part of the book. We are generously provided with several stories that leave us feeling at the same time sad, humbled, and empowered as to what we can do to serve children, women, elderly and men who were forced to lose contact with their roots in order to remain alive in God's kingdom.

This is a book that leaves the reader with essential knowledge, information, and spiritual tools to serve and help those who migrate in order to escape death from the hands of ruthless fellow human beings, or to seek better living conditions after despairing. They endure living in difficult conditions with minimum means of subsistence threatened by illness and death due to malnutrition, harsh weather conditions, poor hygiene, and suffering from dependency and discrimination at all levels of existence.

Nabil Costa
Executive Director,
Lebanese Society for Educational and Social Development

One of every one hundred and thirteen people with whom we share the planet is a refugee, internally displaced, or a migrant on the move. Desperation may drive them to simply cross a border, climb into a small boat, or walk thousands of kilometers through foreign lands. The reaction in many northern countries has been to erect real or figurative walls to keep people out. Rupen Das and Brent Hamoud have made an outstanding contribution to those of us caught between harsh political rhetoric and the gospel teaching of compassion. The authors explain legal definitions of terms like refugee, statelessness, and internal displacement. They also examine the biblical teaching about aliens and strangers that were forced to live outside their ethnic groups and homelands. Each chapter begins with a case study that reminds us that we are dealing with real people. The analysis of the impact of loss of identity and not belonging is compelling and opens our missional understanding of welcoming the stranger.

Gordon King
Canadian Baptist Ministries
Former Member, Immigration and Refugee Board of Canada

In today's world of increasing division and barriers, Rupen Das and Brent Hamoud provide a timely counter-narrative by suggesting that the church's imperative to respond to the needs of "outsiders" comes from the very nature of who God is. By looking more deeply at the theological and personal significance of place and belonging, and illustrated by stories from those who have lived the experience, *Strangers in the Kingdom* reveals the importance of the church's unique role in creating and participating in a place of genuine welcome where people are valued as those made in God's image. Reflecting what I've seen in my work alongside the local church in Lebanon, the very act of welcoming is transformative and allows us the privilege of participating in the nature of a God who crosses divides and chooses to give of himself to welcome us in.

Kezia M'Clelland
Children in Emergencies Programme Specialist, Viva

Strangers in the Kingdom is a profound book that moves the reader deep into the stories and challenges of the displaced. The numbers of those displaced are increasing ever so exponentially, and tragically, each year. The complexities are many, but *Strangers in the Kingdom* reminds us that each life is precious and that God's concern is for all peoples and all nations. The authors provide a refreshing depth of theological sense-making that can inspire us and challenge us as to reach out in compassion and dignity to refugees, migrants and the stateless. The book includes helpful examples of churches and communities welcoming and embracing those who may be strangers, demonstrating God's grace and responding to the human need for belonging. The study questions included in each chapter can only encourage community learning and action. *Strangers in the Kingdom* is a book to thoroughly read and learn from and then keep close by as a comprehensive reference – a refreshing reminder that God gives guidance and strength to care for the poor and to do justice.

Will Postma
Executive Director, The Primate's World Relief and Development Fund

A deeply relevant and timely toolkit that provides both theological and practical insights for the local church to understand and respond to the current crisis of forced migration, as well as with the backlash against migrants, which appears to be on the rise within many receiving communities. Through their reflection on both Old and New Testament texts, Rupen Das and Brent Hamoud make it clear that to walk with those who are newcomers, far from home, or stateless, is to touch a "fundamental aspect of God's intention for creation." Perhaps this book's greatest contribution is to push towards a more profound understanding of the refugee experience, one that moves us away from a theoretical political analysis to a more intimate understanding of the pain of losing one's place, one's roots – essentially all that is familiar and what makes us who we are. Such a loss cannot simply be restored by living in a new "space," but rather the church as a life-giving community is uniquely equipped to help nurture and restore the deep sense of loss experienced by the displaced. Will we heed God's call to love our neighbor as ourselves, and to care for the foreigner in our midst? To do so, argue the authors, is perhaps to experience an essential part of God himself.

Nadia Khouri

Community Health Center Director, Beirut, Lebanon

In an era when wars and persecution have driven more people from their homes than at any other time since World War II, Rupen Das and Brent Hamoud provide a thoroughly engaging investigation to help Jesus-followers consider what responsibilities they have to assist those who have been displaced. Their rich encounters with "displaced sojourners" across the globe have clearly stirred creative turmoil in their own spirituality, and in the crucible of discomfort these courageous authors have wrestled with biblical, theological, and missiological questions earthed in the spectacle of gospel hope they have witnessed in unexpected ways and places.

All followers of Jesus seeking to welcome, serve and learn from displaced people will find this a useful resource enabling them to learn from their experiences and develop ongoing responses that might become even more prophetic in changing times.

Juliet Kilpin

Coordinator, Urban Expression

Peacemaker, Peaceful Borders

Strangers in the Kingdom is both personal and timely. Displacement is our generation's collective tragedy and our reaction will serve to judge us long after we are gone. There have been two major reactions to displacement – fear and ignorance. Das and Hamoud's experience and scholarship help educate and promote compassion for the millions of people who do not have a voice. The issue of displacement is not a "far away" event – refugees and asylum seekers are now our neighbors. It is our responsibility to understand them . . . and love them. I am thankful for the time and energy the authors have spent on this important effort. Indeed, it needs to be read by every Christian, particularly those in the West.

Shane Lakatos
Co-founder of Social Services for the Arab Community (SSFAC)
Toledo, Ohio, USA

Strangers in the Kingdom called hundreds of situations, histories and testimonies of people in need to my mind, brought tears to my eyes and put a fiery passion in my heart, to keep doing work for the love of those in need and, empowered by LOVE that GOD has given me, to involve more people in it!

This book is an eye opener and an instrument of God for helping us learn the correct terminology regarding who the refugees, displaced and migrants are. It is also an aid for understanding, in the theological, missiological and biblical terms, who the strangers are, whom God has called us to love and accept as our own people, motivating us to pray for compassion like his, and for God to open our eyes and let us see as he sees.

Rupen Das and Brent Hamoud did a great job writing this book and I am excited that you have decided to read it. *Strangers in the Kingdom* can change your perspective on life so that you can see people and the world today in the way Jesus sees them – so that the world and the lives of millions of people can be changed by his love and compassion. And my prayer for you, as you read this book, is that you will see that you are essential in this kingdom, the kingdom of God, as a voice for the voiceless.

Cesar Sotomayor
Austrian Baptist Aid

Strangers in the Kingdom

Strangers in the Kingdom

Ministering to Refugees, Migrants, and the Stateless

Rupen Das and Brent Hamoud

Published 2017 by Langham Global Library
An imprint of Langham Publishing
www.langhampublishing.org

Langham Publishing and its imprints are a ministry of Langham Partnership

Langham Partnership
PO Box 296, Carlisle, Cumbria, CA3 9WZ, UK
www.langham.org

ISBNs:
978-1-78368-277-5 Print
978-1-78368-279-9 Mobi
978-1-78368-278-2 ePub
978-1-78368-280-5 PDF

British Library Cataloguing in Publication Data

A catalogue record for this book is available from the British Library
ISBN: 978-1-78368-277-5

Cover & Book Design: projectluz.com

Glimpses of Reality

Today, during the afternoon, while the Croatian Baptist Aid team was preparing vegetable packages for the refugees, they witnessed a death of a three-year-old baby. The baby from Syria died in the hands of her parents. Truly, those were very difficult moments not just for the family but for the whole camp as well. During our four days of work, we got close to the family because we were engaged in conversation and fellowship with them each day. This family suffered a great tragedy today; they lost their child after days of sickness and inefficient medical care. Due to the lack of help, this baby let go its last breath in this world today.

Could the doctors have reacted better? Could the organizations responsible for the camp have done something more to prevent this? How did all this [death of the baby] happen unnoticed by the eyes of the biggest inter-governmental organization in the world for refugees? Why is this [plight of the refugees in Greece] being ignored? Why do people in Europe hate us? Those were just some of the questions asked by the refugees.

Croatian Baptist Aid team in Greece. Email 11 November 2016.

Our refugee families began to feel that maybe they really could live here and feel at home. Suddenly they were able to picture themselves being a part of this community. To slightly change that African saying, "It takes a neighbourhood to welcome a refugee." Because of the "warmth of the welcome," something clicked.

That phrase comes from an interesting longitudinal study, the Refugee Resettlement Project, done by Dr Morton Beiser who is now with Ryerson University. He asked refugees, mostly the Vietnamese boat people, what had helped them integrate well, and they answered that it was the "warmth of the welcome." Isn't that interesting? Employment, housing, English classes – those things are important, but it was a personal, caring connection that was the key to successful integration.

Mary Jo Leddy, refugee advocate and founder of Romero House
in Toronto, Canada. Taken from "A Kolbe Times Interview
with Mary Jo Leddy," *Kolbe Times*, 11 September 2016.

Contents

Foreword

Today in Europe and the Middle East there are unprecedented numbers of people on the move, refugees, migrants, and those who have become "stateless." In the last few years, many fleeing the terrible war in Syria, or the activities of ISIS in the Middle East, or famine and poverty in Africa have begun the perilous journey to Europe, and some from there to North America. The unprecedented numbers arriving in Europe have threatened to overwhelm the ability of governments to respond and have led to questions about what limitations different countries should place on numbers, and whether borders should remain open or closed. Added to these has been a concern that an open door for refugees might allow in those who espouse terrorism. And all this set against a growing populism and nationalist rhetoric that can come across as hostile to "the other who is different from us."

In this situation, many churches in Europe and the Middle East have wanted to respond according to their faith which commands them to "love the stranger" and "love your neighbour," to show Christian hospitality, and to value every human being as a precious gift made in the image of God. In the Baptist communities that I serve in Europe and the Middle East, we have seen many fine examples of churches opening their doors and their hearts to care for the physical, psychological, and spiritual needs of refugees who have often lost everything, and come fearful of the reaction that awaits them. Many refugees and migrants have testified to how they have found welcoming love and acceptance from the Christians they have met.

Churches in their turn have begun to describe the situation not as a "crisis" but to emphasize the "blessing" that refugees have brought to their churches. Often they have been honest about the change to their church life, mission thinking, and openness to the needs of the world that their encounters with refugees have brought them. A few have come alongside individuals as advocates for justice as they pursue their legal case for asylum and the right to remain in the country where they have found refuge.

What has become clear is that this is no short-term crisis. The situation of refugees and migrants being present in large numbers in countries in Europe and the Middle East is set to continue, and churches are challenged to play their part in meeting the medium and long-term needs of refugees and migrants. Some biblical and theological reflection, as well as developing practical experience, now needs to be brought to bear to provide churches with some of the necessary tools to sustain this ministry.

Rupen Das and Brent Hamoud are uniquely qualified to address these practical, biblical, theological, and missiological issues. They are both outstanding Christian leaders who combine professional expertise in humanitarian aid with a highly developed biblical and theological understanding of the issues. In recent times they have both served on the "front line," working with significant numbers of Syrian refugees in Lebanon. Rupen went on to work for the European Baptist Federation as a catalyst and enabler giving vital help to churches and Baptist Unions to increase their effectiveness in reaching out to refugees.

This book will be most helpful to churches and denominational agencies who are serious about increasing their understanding of the current situation and are also working through what the Bible and our faith have to say about those who find themselves on the move as refugees and migrants. As Brent puts it so succinctly in his introduction, "*There is great comfort in knowing that God is not silent on displacement; the Bible speaks to the plight of the refugee, migrant, and stateless individual and invites all to a kingdom of justice, deliverance, and hope.*"

The themes are explored in some depth, and particular attention is paid to the central issue of the loss of "belonging." I found most interesting the discussion of a "theology of place" as it is developed in the Old and New Testaments: the tension between God's affirmation of the importance of our specific settled location in the world and the perspective of God's kingdom which is beyond space and time.

Especially in the last chapter, but also elsewhere, are helpful examples and case studies from the rich experience of the authors that help to root their biblical and theological reflections in the reality of the responses of churches.

Running through the whole book is the conviction of the authors that in this aspect of the mission and ministry of our churches, we should reflect the loving compassion of God for all, and especially for the poor and those who find themselves "strangers." As the authors say in their conclusion, "*In ministering to the vulnerable and marginalized, we minister to God directly.*"

This timely and important book will, I believe, help churches who seek to follow the way of the refugee Christ to be clearer and surer of their motivation for this aspect of sharing in God's mission of love to the world. I warmly commend it.

Rev Tony Peck
General Secretary
European Baptist Federation
Bristol, UK
January 2017

Preface

Fundamental to any definition of spirituality is that it can never be something that can be isolated from the rest of our existence.

David Bosch[1]

Books such as this come out of the turmoil of one's spirituality when the question is what does it mean to be a follower of Christ and a people of God in a world where large numbers of people are forcibly displaced and where others migrate because they are seeking to live life with dignity, something they have been denied. There are competing narratives of why people move and how they should be treated. Unfortunately, an increasing trend towards racism and xenophobia is emerging in many contexts, and the demand to close the borders to unwanted foreigners has become a rallying cry of many people and politicians. There is a very real fear that the present refugee crisis and the increase in migration is leading to terrorism, crime, and a diluting of what people perceive to be their national identity. Others welcome a pluralistic society and the diversity of cultures and experiences it brings, and they embrace it. They see the migration of peoples from one land to another as an inevitable reality of the globalized world we live in.

Does the Bible have anything to say about migration and displacement and how refugees, migrants, and the stateless should be treated? This book is written not only as a work of practical theology but also as a resource for churches and organizations that are seeking to help people impacted by displacement. It is meant to provide a nuanced biblical and theological understanding of how God sees the foreigner and why he is concerned for their well-being, and stories and case studies aim to put a human face to the theology and the biblical studies.

Chapter 1, the introduction, lays the foundation for what will be discussed in the book. A main problem refugees, migrants, and the stateless face is that they find themselves in a place where they do not belong. While in many cases they used to have a home and an identity, their displacement has robbed them of both. They used to be able to meet their own needs, but now they

---

1. David J. Bosch, *A Spirituality of the Road* (Eugene, OR: Wipf and Stock, 1979), 13.

are in unfamiliar places where they struggle to provide for themselves and their families, often while feeling unwanted by the communities around them. Meeting physical needs is critically important, but a compassionate response to those who are displaced must go beyond providing shelter and material needs. They need help to find a way to belong. They need a place to call home again. Chapter 2 looks at the reality of displacement today and identifies the legal definitions that categorize primary categories of displaced peoples. This technical knowledge is essential to the discussion because it gives insight to the specific situations of the displaced, what their needs are, and how their suffering should be addressed.

Chapter 3 focuses on biblical teachings by exploring the issue of the vulnerable foreigners in ancient Israel and the laws established to govern their treatment. Chapter 4 looks at the issue of the foreigners and migrants in first-century Palestine who had no social networks to help them in times of need and Jesus's teachings and example of how they should be treated. We then look at how the early church engaged with those who were in need among them and those outside their community.

Chapter 5 frames the theological issue of displacement and the problem of not belonging. Chapter 6 explores the missiological dimensions of ministering to those who are displaced. The model here is in the incarnation, God entering into a world of turmoil and evil because he cares about what happens to the people he created. He feels deeply about how evil has warped his creation; rather than walking away and excluding them from his presence, he embraces them and provides them the opportunity of experiencing his care, mercy, and compassion.

Chapter 7 looks at various ministries to the displaced, specifically in local churches. Some of the examples and case studies in this chapter from the Middle East, Europe, and Canada are based on the experiences of both of us and our colleagues. The geographic focus entails no intention of diminishing the excellent work being done by NGOs, mission agencies, churches, and individuals in other parts of the world. Displacement is a global reality, and many examples exist of outstanding responses by faith communities. However, the recent crisis in the Middle East has challenged churches to become directly involved in addressing the humanitarian needs of refugees on a scale not seen in recent memory. We want to highlight the fact that local churches, and not just international NGOs and local civil society, do have a place in ministering to people in need.

At the end of each chapter are questions that a church or group reflecting on the issues in this book could discuss. Chapter 7 provides some guidelines for local churches who would like to minister to refugees and the stateless. However, this book is not a manual on how to minister to the displaced. There are excellent resources available from the United Nations and other organizations on the specific details of how to respond to the needs of refugees and the stateless, and some of these are listed in chapter 7. The objective of this book is to look at Scripture and our world and to think theologically about what is required from God's people to reveal the hidden kingdom and the God we worship, especially to those who have no place to call home. The focus of this book is understanding those who have lost their homes, fled their countries, and lost their identity in the process, and how to help them find another place they can call home and experience the blessings of God.

Quite a bit has been written about migrants, ministering to migrants, and migrant churches. Rather than trying to duplicate existing work, this book will primarily look at the need for migrants to belong again and find a new home – the same need of refugees and the stateless. This is by no means a comprehensive theological study, but we do aim to facilitate discussion and encourage faith communities to seize the opportunities to be a light of Christ in the face of a massive crisis.

Our prayer for you and us in the work we do among the poor, the refugees, and others who have lost their sense of home and feel like they do not belong, is Psalm 90:17:

> *May the favour of the Lord our God rest on us;*
>
> *establish the work of our hands for us –*
>
> *yes, establish the work of our hands.*

Acknowledgements

This book emerges out of the questions, tensions, and problems of the refugee crisis facing the world today, and more specifically from the midst of the Syrian conflict. Having worked for Christian non-governmental organizations (NGOs) for much of my career, the Syrian crisis made me ask yet again what is a Christian response to the refugees and is there a place for the local church in a humanitarian response addressing those who are displaced.

It has been a delight to work on this book with Brent Hamoud, as we both realized we had been asking similar questions and there was much synergy in our thinking. We bring complementary experiences to this project, which has resulted in a more balanced and fuller understanding of the needs of the displaced – refugees, migrants, and the stateless.

I am grateful for the partnerships and conversations with various organizations, church unions, and countless individuals who have made me aware of the issues, as well as showing me what compassion looks like through the local church. In particular, I want to acknowledge Nabil Costa and the team at the Lebanese Society for Educational and Social Development (LSESD); Thomas Klammt at the German Baptist Union; Daniel Rasberg with InterAct Sweden; Cesar Sotomayor and David Bunce at Project Gemeinde in Vienna, Austria; and Igor Bandura, Vladimir Ivanickiy, and Guennadi Khijniak with the Ukrainian Baptist Union. Loralyn Lind in Dauphin, Manitoba, and Paul and Kelly Carline in Saint John, New Brunswick, Canada were very gracious in sharing their experiences with resettling new refugees. The leadership of the European Baptist Federation (EBF), Tony Peck and Helle Liht, and Terry Smith, the head of Canadian Baptist Ministries (CBM), continue to provide me opportunities to be involved in ministering to refugees and the internally displaced. It was these contexts that allowed us to experiment with new ideas and ask the questions that led to this book. I want to thank Gary Nelson, president of Tyndale University College and Seminary in Toronto, and Stuart Blythe, the rector of the International Baptist Theological Study Center (IBTSC) in Amsterdam for providing me with academic homes where I can continue to research and write.

I am always appreciative of Vivian Doub and the team at Langham Global Library for facilitating the whole process of ensuring that all the pieces were in place for this book to be published.

I want to acknowledge my wife, Mamta, who through her infinite patience and love allows me the space to think and write.

Encounters over the past many years with refugees and others who are displaced have been life changing for me. "When refugees have a name and a face and a story, we begin to know who they are, and who *we* are."[1]

Rupen Das
Amsterdam, Netherlands
2017

We must be concerned about the problem of displacement because (1) it is a global crisis facing millions of individuals, and (2) we live in an unstable world where every individual is one political conflict, natural disaster, or personal tragedy away from finding herself or himself displaced from all that is familiar and secure. There is great comfort in knowing that God is not silent on displacement; the Bible speaks to the plight of the refugee, migrant, and stateless individual and invites all to a kingdom of justice, deliverance, and hope. My prayer is that this humble resource will stir our hearts to compassion and open our eyes to the opportunities of the kingdom emerging around us today.

I am grateful for the Institute of Middle East Studies (IMES) at the Arab Baptist Theological Seminary (ABTS) for providing an academic program that gave me the tools and space to explore the themes of this book. I offer a sincere thank you to Rupen Das for supervising my graduate thesis on statelessness and inviting me to join him in writing this book. I also extend heartfelt thanks to the partner churches, family members, and friends who allow me to dedicate my time and energy to creating places of belonging for at-risk children and youth in Lebanon.

I owe much to the family members who have provided a legacy of selfless compassion towards the displaced: to my grandparents who spent over half a century serving refugees and at-risk children in Lebanon; my mother who throughout my upbringing in the Twin Cities, Minnesota, involved me in her

1. "A Kolbe Times Interview with Mary Jo Leddy," *Kolbe Times* (11 September 2016), http://www.kolbetimes.com/a-kolbe-times-interview-with-mary-jo-leddy/.

ongoing personal ministry to refugees and immigrants; and to my father whose personal testimony reveals that God is near to the displaced and working for our good.

For this book and everything else, I thank my wonderful wife, Ruth, for her friendship, love, and unwavering support.

I am also thankful for the friends and loved ones who, in their encounters with displacement, have shown me new dimensions of faith and hope in God. Particular appreciation for Tarek Agile, who in his own situation introduced me to the problem of statelessness while demonstrating high character during his multi-year struggle to gain official belonging in this world. And to my many Hamoud family members who face their daily struggle of displacement with great courage, never losing hope that they will one day return to our beloved Syria. These special people are a true inspiration, and I am blessed to be a small part of their stories.

Brent Hamoud
Beirut, Lebanon
2017

PART I

Foundations for Ministries to the Displaced

1

Introduction

All of us can draw inspiration from the courage and perseverance in overcoming adversity and building a better future, as demonstrated by millions of refugees. Many endure enormous suffering without losing hope, and find the strength to overcome despair and start a new life against seemingly overwhelming odds.

Kofi Annan, former United Nations secretary general[1]

Saadya was born in Somalia's capital, Mogadishu, after it had been destroyed and was controlled by various warlords.[2] *When she was age ten, her father, brother, and sister were killed when they were caught in the middle of a battle near their home. After a few months of struggling to survive, Saadya's mother made the decision to leave Somalia. The two of them walked through various rebel-controlled areas to northern Somalia and then onto Djibouti, carrying what little they could and begging for food along the way. They found a boat of smugglers who were going across the Gulf of Aden to Yemen and paid all the money they had to join them. Halfway across the Gulf, they ran out of fuel, and the smugglers abandoned the boat, causing them to drift aimlessly. Fortunately, they were rescued by a ship, and the crew helped them reach Yemen safely.*

Having no money, Saadya and her mother lived on the streets depending on others for food and shelter wherever they could find it. Sometimes her mother found work, usually as a servant or a labourer. Finally, after four years someone

1. United Nations Information Service (UNIS), "It Takes Courage to Be a Refugee United Nations Commemorates World Refugee Day on 20 June," 2005, http://www.unis.unvienna.org/unis/pressrels/2005/unisinf84.html.

2. The names of individuals and some of the details of their stories have been changed so they cannot be identified and put at risk.

told them to approach the United Nations High Commissioner for Refugees (UNHCR) for help. They applied for resettlement. After a further three-year wait, they were resettled in North America in a place where there were other Somali immigrants. While Saadya and her mother had lost their family and everything else they had, they were able to start life afresh.

There are moments in history that the world remembers. In the last few decades, the liberation of Bangladesh, the Rwandan genocide, the horrors of the Bosnian conflict, the civil wars in Sierra Leone and Liberia, and the Iraq wars have resulted in human suffering on such a massive scale that the world has had to take notice. Today the humanitarian crises in Syria, Iraq, Afghanistan, and northern Nigeria (and in so many other places) are overwhelming the capacity of humanitarian agencies to cope with the large number of refugees and internally displaced persons. According to the United Nations, wars and persecution have driven more people from their homes today than at any other time since World War II. Four times more people are displaced than were a decade earlier. United Nations high commissioner for refugees Filippo Grandi states, "At sea, a frightening number of refugees and migrants are dying each year. On land, people fleeing war are finding their way blocked by closed borders. Closing borders does not solve the problem."[3]

Migration and forced displacement are defining this moment of history. What is challenging is the scale of the displacements and the inability of the international community to cope. Grandi writes, "The willingness of nations to work together not just for refugees but for the collective human interest is what's being tested today, and it's this spirit of unity that badly needs to prevail."[4]

Human History Is a History of Migration

Migration has been a reality since the beginning of time. Anthropologists and scholars trace the movement of tribes and peoples across continents to solve the mysteries of how we have arrived in the places we are. Some people moved in search of better land and climatic conditions in order to survive. Others were

3. Adrian Edwards, "Global Forced Displacement Hits Record High," UNHCR, 20 June 2016, http://www.unhcr.org/news/latest/2016/6/5763b65a4/global-forced-displacement-hits-record-high.html.

4. UNHCR, *Global Trends – Forced Displacement in 2015* (Geneva: United Nations, 2015), 8.

forcibly displaced as a result of wars and conflicts. Far too many have been trafficked in slave trades across countries, continents, and oceans, and others moved when their land was unable to support growing populations. Yet many have set out in quest of new opportunities and the prospect of new lives in distant lands. Though the historical causes of human migration have varied, all people exist somewhere because people at one point have moved there from somewhere else. It is a phenomenon of human history that permeates the biblical narrative. Old Testament scholar and missiologist Christopher Wright observes:

> Migration runs like a thread through the whole Bible narrative. People on the move (for all kinds of reasons) are so much part of the fabric of the story that we hardly notice it as a major feature. Indeed, when the text actually points out that YHWH, God of Israel, has been involved in the migrations of peoples other than Israel, some Bible translations put that affirmation in parentheses – as though to separate it off from the main story, even though it is an integral part of the theological context of the story. YHWH is the God of all nations and all their historical migrations and settlements. (Deut 2:10–12, 20–23)[5]

Yet the idea of migration has been widely ignored by theologians. Daniel Groody at the University of Notre Dame writes, "Theology, however, is almost never mentioned in major works or at centers of migration studies. . . . Even among theologians the topic of migration is largely undocumented."[6] While there is research and literature on migrant churches, there is considerably less theological exploration of the phenomena of displacement (the core tragedy of the forced migrant, refugees, and the stateless). Often the reasons for why Christians should respond to the needs of the displaced invariably mention that Jesus was a refugee and that the Old Testament says we should take care of the vulnerable foreigners in our midst. The question is whether a few instructions and instances provide the breadth of what Scripture teaches concerning the foreigners among us, or is there something more? Is it possible that compassionate responses to the outsider touch a fundamental aspect of

---

5. Christopher Wright, "An Old Testament Perspective," paper presented at the Stott-Bedaiko Forum "The Refugee Crisis: Our Common Human Condition," Oxford University, 2016, 1.

6. Daniel G. Groody, *Crossing the Divide: Foundations of a Theology of Migration and Refugees*, Monograph 15 (Oxford: Crowther Centre Monographs, 2010), 6–7.

God's intention for creation – that through such responses he is communicating who he is?

This idea of being migrants, pilgrims, and strangers is so foundational within Scripture that it defines how the people of God should live. Wright states that, since Abraham, the notion of sojourning has now become part of our theological, historical, and spiritual DNA.[7] It also challenges our understanding of citizenship and identity in this world; the people of God now boast a claim to an irrevocable citizenship in a heavenly kingdom and identify themselves as the followers of an eternal king regardless of who they are or what happens to them here on earth.

Migration has become one of the foremost issues of the twenty-first century as the presence of refugees and migrants becomes a growing political and social issue globally. Some people view the "outsider" with deep fear as a threat to national and personal security. They cite various acts of terrorism and incidents of sexual violence as arguments for closing borders and rejecting foreigners. They also see the issue as an economic threat. Some worry that jobs will be lost since migrants sometimes undermine local workers by working for lower wages. The race, ethnicity, and religion of refugees and migrants often raise heated discourse about the nature of national identity, and there is now widespread debate over what it means to be European, American, or Australian.

The debate is not limited to the West. Countries like Lebanon, Jordan, Kenya, and Pakistan (among many others) are asking similar questions: How and where do foreigners fit in the existing social and political arrangements that our citizens have between themselves? How do we define ourselves as a country? Having new neighbours who look different and believe differently can be seen as a threat to one's identity and well-being. These fears are often real and grounded in legitimate concerns; the reality of our globalized world is that the insecurity and crises in one country can have direct implications in other parts of the world. These concerns cannot be directly dismissed, and we are increasingly witnessing their force in influencing politics and social policy in many different contexts.

Migration as a Blessing

In the midst of the heated debates about migration taking place around the world are inspiring movements of Christian faith communities taking

7. Wright, "Old Testament Perspective," 2.

compassionate approaches. Many churches see ministering to the displaced as a prophetic act that is central to biblical witness. As society is tempted to view foreigners with fear and respond to their arrival with attack, exclusion, and marginalization, many churches are working to protect and help the vulnerable. In doing so they are revealing the reality of an invisible kingdom where the lonely, the broken, and those in need are valued and cared for. They are providing a demonstration of compassion in the spirit of the Great Commandment's call to love your neighbour as yourself.

Many Christian faith communities likewise see refugees and migrants as a missional opportunity. As many traditional institutional churches have retreated in their commitment to global missions, they see the presence of foreigners in their communities as God bringing the mission field to them. Ironically, the impact of refugees and migrants joining churches is changing the churches themselves. Not only are a significant number of refugees and migrants becoming followers of Christ across Europe, church leaders in contexts where large numbers of migrants have embraced Christ attest to the fact that migrant churches contribute to the vitality of worship and Christian life to denominations that have been stagnant for decades. In some denominations in Europe, church growth is almost completely attributable to the growth of the migrant churches. Church historian Phillip Jenkins writes,

> Yet a great many other European immigrants are Christian, and they raise the prospect of a revitalized Christian presence on European soil. . . . Southern influence grows through two distinct but related phenomena. In some areas, Third World churches undertake actual mission work in secularized North America and especially Europe. Commonly, though, evangelism is an incidental by-product of the activities of immigrant churches, an important phenomenon given the large African and Asian communities domiciled in Europe. . . . When we measure the declining strength of Christianity in Europe, we must remember how much leaner the statistics would be if not for the recent immigrants and their children – the new Europeans.[8]

Displaced individuals, victims who have lost their homes and communities, are finding in many churches a welcoming sense of community that allows them to experience belonging again. Migrants and refugees, foreigners who

8. Philip Jenkins, *The Next Christendom: The Coming of Global Christianity* (New York: Oxford University Press, 2007), 113, 115.

are away from all that is familiar to them – lost and alone in their new country – seem to be much more open to God in their desperation than they were in their home countries. Missiological researcher Jenny McGill writes,

> Migration blesses insofar as it enables the person to experience God and thus experience a change of self-understanding (Gen. 32:22–32; Ex. 3). The nearness of God is perhaps no more acutely felt than during an experience of physical displacement, and this nearness is always a migration on God's part, for God ultimately identifies with human suffering (Is. 63:9; Heb. 2:14–18). . . . God's companionship in suffering signifies that humanity is deeply cherished by God.[9]

Though full of opportunities, ministering to foreigners and others who do not belong to one's faith or national community is indeed a challenge. When confronted with inviting foreigners and those who are culturally different to become part of God's people, most churches struggle with maintaining their identity – of how they have defined themselves over the years. They find themselves forced out of their comfort zone, moving away from traditions that are familiar to them. Yet they desire to be relevant by being compassionate to the vulnerable. German theologian Jürgen Moltmann describes this tension as being between *identity* and *relevance*, a dilemma that every church in every generation faces.[10] A church's identity is defined by its history, beliefs, and practices. This sense of history gives them meaning and stability. However, churches exist in a changing and dynamic world. Responding to human need and inviting those who are different into their community will result in changing who faith communities are as a church.

While forced displacement is never God's primary intention, McGill writes, "God utilizes the migration of people, forced and voluntary, to shape the identity of God's people and the identity of those who do not know God."[11] She uses the examples of Joseph in Egypt and Daniel in Babylon, both in forced displacements and both by their faith and lifestyle challenging the preconceived notions and worldviews of the kings and elite about who God is. While they may not have moved the leaders to worship the living God, McGill writes, "This presence of difference disrupted the status quo of the community's assumed

9. Jenny McGill, *Religious Identity and Cultural Negotiation: Toward a Theology of Christian Identity in Migration* (Eugene, OR: Pickwick, 2016), 204–205.

10. Jürgen Moltmann, *The Crucified God* (London: SCM, 1974), 3.

11. McGill, *Religious Identity*, 199.

identities."[12] Migration and displacement, especially of the people of God, can be seen as a blessing to the host nations, as the prophet Jeremiah encouraged the ancient Israelites in exile to see. "Seek the peace and prosperity of the city to which I have carried you into exile. Pray to the LORD for it, because if it prospers, you too will prosper" (Jer 29:7).

The Need to Belong

Ministries to refugees and other victims of displacement commonly focus on serving physical needs. Initiatives and programs invest in providing shelter, clothing, food, and access to healthcare. They seek to ensure that children go to school and that the special needs of the elderly and disabled are met. Some programs focus on employment so that refugees can take care of their families. In Western refugee host countries, churches and social service agencies provide language training and programs to help newcomers navigate the cultural, legal, and social challenges of their new country of residence. These are critical programs and help to improve the well-being of refugee, migrant, and stateless individuals. Yet in the midst of providing such services, some of the deepest of human needs are left untouched.

Many things are lost in the nightmare of displacement. Homes and villages are destroyed, families are separated, lives are lost, and dreams for the future are crushed. But one of the harshest losses facing the displaced is the loss of belonging to a community. Their identity and sense of self are undermined. They struggle to find meaning in who they are based on where they come from, the jobs they have, the family or tribe they belong to, or the lands and possessions they own. Many even face a serious legal loss of identity as the process of displacement robs them of their nationality or their ability to prove their own official status in this world. At nearly all levels of existence, displacement undercuts the security of belonging.

Migration and displacement are a part of the biblical narrative because Scripture looks at the foreigner and is very concerned with the question, "*What does it mean for human beings to not belong?*" The vulnerability of the outsider proceeds from the problem of not belonging. It is because they do not belong that they are vulnerable and in need. Scripture addresses the loss and pain of being an outsider and addresses it in the here and now of created time by urging the people of God to respond to the human needs of the "other." Scripture

12. Ibid.

ultimately elevates above all things a heavenly citizenship, the privilege of belonging to a family and household in an eternal kingdom.

Terms such as *refugees*, *migrants* and *stateless* are not found in Scripture. These are modern categories denoting people in specific types of situations in our global system of nation-states, terminology used to describe people who have a problematic relationship with their places. They are usually people who have moved from their homes, either voluntarily or involuntarily, and lack a secure sense of belonging in the places where they now live. However, the idea of a foreigner who is alone, who has been excluded from society, is experiencing poverty, and has no one to protect him or her is an ancient reality. These vulnerable individuals, just as the poor, seem to be of special concern to God.

In order to minister to those who have suffered displacement, it is important to understand that the stateless, migrants, and refugees are not simply objects of pity that require our generosity and charity. The starting point instead is the realization that all human beings are made in the image of God (Gen 1:26–27); each person displays in some mysterious way the beauty, nature, and character of the Creator. He who created a complex universe and a beautiful earth filled with colors and variety did the same with human beings. God does not discriminate between the races. All people reflect who God is – his image – which is illuminated, not limited, by ethnicity, color, and gender. Our failure to recognize and celebrate this foundational truth has led to a history of discrimination, violence, and injustice. Instead of defining ourselves in relationship to our Creator, we create ethnicity, tribe, religion, and nationality, and we resort to these human terms to define who we are, who is worthy of dignity and value, and who is not. We continually succumb to the temptation to differentiate and separate from others who are not like us.

Yet God's concern is for all peoples, all nations. Even if they are in rebellion against him now, God is in the process of redeeming all of his creation. All nations will one day worship him.

> *All the nations you have made*
> *will come and worship before you, Lord;*
> *they will bring glory to your name.* (Ps 86:9)

The Sovereign Lord, who has brought his people Israel home from exile, has promised that he will bring still other people to join them (Is 56:8).

> *The kingdom of the world has become*
> *the kingdom of our Lord and of his Messiah,*
> *and he will reign for ever and ever.* (Rev 11:15)

In the kingdom of God there are no foreigners who are excluded or unwelcome. All can respond to the invitation and become part of his kingdom.

This book is an attempt to understand God's concern for the foreigner – the refugee, the stateless, and the migrant in our midst. How are God's people called to demonstrate the reality of the kingdom by showing compassion to them? This is an exploration into the heart and mind of God to try to see how he sees the foreigner and then to discern our responsibility as his people.

Questions for Reflection and Discussion

1. What do you think it means to not belong?
2. What do you think *it feels like* to not belong?
3. Are there migrants, refugees, and stateless people in your community? How would you find out who they are and where they live?
4. Are these people accepted by the majority community? In what ways do you see that they are accepted, and in what ways do you see that they are not?
5. Think of a time when you faced the feeling of not belonging. How can this experience inform you about the situations of the displaced today?

2

The Global Context

While every refugee's story is different and their anguish personal, they all share a common thread of uncommon courage – the courage to not only survive, but to persevere and rebuild their shattered lives.

Antonio Guterrez, former United Nations high commissioner for refugees and current UN secretary general[1]

Maryum and Mohammad owned a small business in Aleppo, Syria, when the war started.[2] In the beginning the war did not affect them; they could only hear the bombs and guns in the distance. But slowly it started coming closer. One day a bomb exploded outside their house, almost destroying it and killing some people they knew in their neighbourhood. Mohammad says, "By the grace of God none of us were injured." With so much of the city around them destroyed, they realized that they could not continue living there, so they decided to leave. It was a very difficult decision as they had many family members in the city.

To avoid the militias and the army, Maryum and Mohammad left at night with their two little children and walked along trails, away from the main roads. It took them two weeks to reach Lebanon. They had some money and hardly any food. They finally found some other people from their neighbourhood in Aleppo who allowed them to share their tent and food till they could set up their own tent. They constructed their crude accommodation out of some plastic sheeting that they bought and other materials they found in the garbage.

1. Quoted in David Winter, Rachel Brown, Stephanie Goins, and Clare Mason, *Trauma, Survival and Resilience in War Zones: The Psychological Impact of War in Sierra Leone and Beyond* (London: Routledge, 2016), 133.

2. The names of individuals and some of the details of their stories have been changed so they cannot be identified and put at risk.

Mohammad is unable to find any work because there are so many refugees in Lebanon. They get some food from the UN through one organization. It is not enough, but they manage by eating one meal a day. In winter they struggle because it is so cold and they have only one stove. Sometimes they don't have enough fuel and have to borrow from friends. What money they brought with them is almost gone. Maryum says, "It is hard to see the children growing without enough food. They are not able to attend school either. We don't know what the future will bring."

The Crisis in Context

The world seems to have crossed an unseen threshold. In their 2015 annual report, the United Nation's agency responsible for refugees (UNHCR) reported that the number of people forcibly displaced has reached 65.3 million.[3] This is the highest global amount since World War II. It amounts to one in every 113 persons in the world today, with nearly 34,000 persons being forced to flee from their homes every single day.[4]

Of the 65.3 million displaced, 21.3 million (32.6 percent) are refugees who have fled from their countries because of conflict, violence, or persecution. Ten million of the 65.3 million are stateless, meaning they have been deprived nationality and claim no membership to any nation-state. They lack many basics such as education, healthcare, employment, and freedom of movement. Three countries – Somalia (1.1 million), Afghanistan (2.7 million), and Syria (4.9 million) – produce large numbers of refugees.[5]

These numbers are no doubt staggering, but like so many statistics their meaning is limited because they are rarely connected to people we know or care about. We are often unable to relate to the trauma and agony faced by the people numbered here. Statistics alone fail to tell the story of the terrified families who suddenly become destitute, of children who have lost their parents, of young widows trying to raise their families on their own with no source of income, and of the elderly and disabled – all of whom somehow no longer belong anywhere. Numbers do not communicate the nightmare that

3. UNHCR, "Figures at a Glance: Global Trends 2015," http://www.unhcr.org/en-us/figures-at-a-glance.html. Gathering displacement statistics is problematic with many shortcomings in methodology. It is widely believed that actual numbers of displaced are higher than the reported figures.

4. Ibid.

5. Ibid.

occurs when an individual who has been firmly rooted in his or her home for a lifetime suddenly becomes a non-citizen of the world. The scale of displacement and the number of people suffering is no secret, yet the world falls short time and time again in finding real solutions to solvable problems.

The displacement crisis engulfing the world right now is by no means a new phenomenon. The past century has witnessed numerous waves of refugees fleeing conflict, persecution, destruction of homes and livelihoods, and death. Some of the larger displacements in recent history have already largely escaped our collective memory. These include the following:[6]

1940–45	40 million people were displaced during World War II.
1945–50	Post-World War II, 1 million Belarusians, Ukrainians, and Russians were displaced, and 13 million Germans were expelled from Poland, Czechoslovakia, and the Soviet Union.
1947	14 million Indians and Pakistanis were displaced during partition of the Indian subcontinent during the time of independence.
1948–50	750,000 Palestinians were displaced from what became the State of Israel.
1954–56	1 million (mainly Roman Catholics) were displaced from North Vietnam to South Vietnam during the communist repressions in North Vietnam.
1960	1.2 million Algerians were displaced internally and to Morocco and Tunisia during the Algerian War of Independence.
1967	The Biafra conflict in Nigeria displaced 2 million, mostly internally.
1971	Bangladesh war displaced 10 million refugees.
1979	Soviet invasion of Afghanistan displaced 6.3 million refugees.
1976–1992	Mozambique war displaced 5.7 million.

6. Lydia DePillis, Kulwant Saluja, and Denise Lu. "A Visual Guide to 75 Years of Major Refugee Crises Around the World," *The Washington Post*, 21 December 2015, https://www.washingtonpost.com/graphics/world/historical-migrant-crisis/.

1989	Civil wars in Central America (Nicaragua, El Salvador, and Guatemala) displaced 2 million.
1994	Rwandan genocide resulted in 3.5 million internally displaced and refugees.
1994–95	Balkans conflict displaced 2.5 million.
2012–15	891,000 Burmese (mainly Rohingyas) were persecuted, internally displaced, denied citizenship, or made refugees.
2011–2016	12.6 million Syrians were internally displaced and made refugees by civil war.
1964–2015	The long running civil conflict in Colombia has resulted in 5.8 million internally displaced.

It would seem from the media headlines that the flows of refugees into Europe, North America, and Australia have reached crisis proportions. Yet the reality is that non-Western countries are bearing the brunt of hosting the majority of refugees. Of the total number of displaced persons, North America only hosts 12 percent and Europe 6 percent. The Middle East and North Africa host 39 percent of the total number of displaced, with sub-Saharan Africa carrying the burden for 29 percent and Asia 14 percent. While some Western countries may complain about being flooded by refugees and migrants, 82 percent of all refugees globally are being hosted by non-Western countries. The countries hosting the greatest numbers of displaced people are Turkey (2.5 million), Pakistan (1.6 million), Lebanon (1.1 million), Iran (979,400), Ethiopia (736,100), and Jordan (664,100).[7] These are mostly poor to middle income countries whose resources to respond to the humanitarian needs have been stretched to the limit.

Types of Displacement and Legal Definitions

The terminology used to describe people who face displacement can often be confusing. There may be questions as to whether a particular displaced person is a migrant or a refugee or in another category. While these terms and categories are critical to our understanding of displacement, especially for those who are providing assistance, the bigger picture is that all displaced persons (either voluntarily or forcibly displaced) are people who suffer because they

7. Ibid.

find themselves in a place where they do not belong. They are *non-citizens* in the countries where they live. The United Nations describes non-citizens in these terms:

> A non-citizen is a person who has not been recognized as having effective links to the country where he or she is located. There are different groups of non-citizens, including permanent residents, migrants, refugees, asylum seekers, victims of trafficking, foreign students, temporary visitors, other kinds of non-immigrants and stateless people. While each of these groups may have rights based on separate legal regimes, the problems faced by most, if not all, non-citizens are very similar. These common concerns affect approximately 175 million individuals worldwide – or 3 percent of the world's population.[8]

It is important to understand the technical terms for displacement and their implications. *Why* people are forced out of their homes and *how* they were displaced determines the legal category to which they belong. These categories define their status under international law and also determine whether they are entitled to protection and assistance.

Refugees

Not everyone who is forced to leave their home is *legally* considered a refugee. According to international law, three criteria are used to judge whether a person is a refugee or not.[9] Refugees are people who (1) have a well-founded fear of persecution because of their race, religion, nationality, membership in a particular social group, or political opinion; (2) are outside their country of origin; and (3) are unable or unwilling to avail themselves of the protection of that country, or return there, because of their fear of persecution.

Once people *have crossed an international border*, they can then apply to the appropriate authorities for protection and assistance as refugees under international law.[10] Most refugees are registered and legally protected. Others, because of fear or other reasons, may choose not to register. As a result, they

---

8. UNHCR, *The Rights of Non-Citizens* (Geneva: United Nations, 2006), 5.

9. Article I, Refugee Convention, "Convention and Protocol Relating to the Status of Refugees" (Geneva: UNHCR 1951).

10. On the very rare occasion people may be deemed refugees before they have left their own country.

do not have access to legal protection, nor can they access humanitarian help to which they would be entitled if they were registered.

A term that is often heard is *asylum seekers*. These are people who have left their country and are seeking protection (asylum) in another country because they feel they are under threat in their home country. If their application for refugee status is granted, they then cease to be an asylum seeker and become a legal refugee and have access to all entitled benefits and protections. If their request is not granted, they will either be returned (voluntarily or forcibly) to their home country, or they risk becoming stateless and disappearing into the world of undocumented illegal migrants in the country.

Internally Displaced Persons (IDP)

People who are forcibly displaced from their homes but *do not cross* an international border and, for whatever reason, remain within their country are considered internally displaced persons (IDPs). While there is no international law that protects them, the United Nations has drafted guiding principles that it uses to monitor and hold national governments accountable to protect the internally displaced. This sometimes proves to be a challenge, especially if the national government is responsible for persecuting and displacing people in the first place.

The definition of an IDP as provided by the Guiding Principles on Internal Displacement is the following:

> Internally displaced persons are persons or groups of persons who have been forced or obliged to flee or to leave their homes or places of habitual residence, in particular as a result of or in order to avoid the effects of armed conflict, situations of generalized violence, violations of human rights or natural or human-made disasters, and who have not crossed an internationally recognized State border.[11]

Statelessness Persons

Statelessness is a particular kind of displacement that leaves its victims without any place of official belonging in this world. Nationality is a basic human

11. Annex, No. 2. Office for the Coordination of Humanitarian Affairs (OCHA), "Guiding Principles on Internal Displacement" (New York: United Nations, 1998).

right that most take for granted.[12] However, there are estimated to be more than ten million individuals living in this world who do not have any formal membership to a nation-state and who are among the world's most vulnerable.[13] The working definition of *statelessness* comes from the "Convention Relating to the Status of Stateless Persons" of 1954 which defines a stateless person as someone "who is not considered as a national by any State under the operation of its law."[14] In other words, the stateless are individuals who, for whatever reason, have no official membership to a nation-state and therefore do not experience the rights, privileges, and protections of citizenship.

The stateless fall into two primary categories: *de jure* (in law) and *de facto* (in fact). *De jure* statelessness occurs when someone does not qualify for nationality under any government's laws and therefore has no possible claim to citizenship.[15] They do not have a legal pathway to obtain nationality to any nation-state. These people can include groups who were excluded from nationality when new states were formed (such as numerous Kurdish, Bedouin, and Gypsy groups in the Middle East) or those who endure blatant discrimination from governments (such as the Rohingya in Burma or Bidoon in Kuwait). De facto statelessness results when people have a claim to formal nationality but do not enjoy access to it, thus leaving them "unable to rely on their country of nationality for protection."[16] Such individuals cannot "obtain proof of their nationality, residency or other means of qualifying for citizenship

---

12. Amendment 15 in the Universal Declaration of Human Rights states, "Everyone has the right to a nationality. No one shall be arbitrarily deprived of his nationality nor denied the right to change his nationality." United Nations, "The Universal Declaration of Human Rights," *United Nations* (New York, NY, 1948), http://www.ohchr.org/EN/UDHR/Documents/UDHR_Translations/eng.pdf.

13. The UNHCR claims the figure of ten million global stateless, although researchers estimate a higher population of fifteen million stateless individuals. One reason for the lesser figure is that "UNHCR's statistical reporting on statelessness excludes stateless persons who also fall within the protection mandates of other UN Agencies (at present, only the UN Relief and Works Agency – UNRWA), and those who also come under other UNHCR protection mandates (such as refugees, IDPs or asylum seekers)." Institute on Statelessness and Inclusion, *The World's Stateless* (Oisterwijk, The Netherlands: Wolf Legal Publishers, 2014), 7, 35.

14. UNHCR, "Convention Relating to the Status of Stateless Persons," 1954, http://www.ohchr.org/Documents/ProfessionalInterest/stateless.pdf, 3.

15. Brad K. Blitz, *Forced Migration Policy Briefing 3: Statelessness, Protection and Equality* (Oxford: Oxford Department of International Development, University of Oxford, 2009), 7.

16. Laura van Waas, *Nationality Matters: Statelessness under International Law.* Dissertation (Tilburg: University of Tilburg, 2008), 20.

and may be excluded from the formal state."[17] This can result when a child's birth is never registered, which is a major issue for babies born to refugees. It is also important to note that statelessness can result when nation-states inflict gender discrimination in nationality laws and deny women the right of passing citizenship to their children, as is the case in Lebanon and Syria.

Statelessness is an acute form of displacement that can result from a variety of circumstances, many of which do not involve forced migration. While refugees face a heightened threat of statelessness, refugees are usually not stateless, and stateless individuals are usually not refugees. The majority of stateless individuals have never left their country of residence, but, without official nationality, they are unable to claim fundamental rights or enjoy the most basic of human opportunities. They are technically foreigners everywhere in this world and essentially do not belong anywhere. Stateless people struggle to enjoy the most basic of life experiences such as gaining employment, attending school, registering marriages and children, accessing healthcare, travelling, and many others. Without the protection of citizenship, they are effectively without rights and vulnerable to a host of human rights abuses and psychological distress.

Migrants

Terms like *migrants* and *refugees* are used quite loosely, and unfortunately at times are used interchangeably. However, the United Nations has created a very specific distinguishing definition. A migrant worker is a "person who is to be engaged, is engaged or has been engaged in a remunerated activity in a State of which he or she is not a national." Their broader definition of migrants is the following: "The term 'migrant' in article 1.1 (a) should be understood as covering all cases where the decision to migrate is taken freely by the individual concerned, for reasons of 'personal convenience' and without intervention of an external compelling factor."[18] The basic difference between migrants and refugees is that migrants have chosen by their own free will to leave their

17. Blitz, *Forced Migration Policy Briefing*, 1. Some examples are Dominicans of Haitian descent; children of foreign domestic workers in Hong Kong who are not granted citizenship in Hong Kong nor by the mother's home country; Palestinians in Lebanon; many descendants of Arab nomads in Kuwait; and Bhutanese refugees in Nepal who have neither Nepali nor Bhutanese citizenship.

18. United Nations General Assembly, "International Convention on the Protection of the Rights of All Migrant Workers and Members of Their Families (CMW). Resolution 45/158 of 18 December 1990" (New York: United Nations, 1990).

home to seek opportunities or a better life in a country other than their own. Refugees, on the other hand, are those who have been forced to leave their home for another country because of violence or persecution.

There are legal migrants and illegal migrants. Legal migrants are protected by the laws of the country where they live and work, while illegal migrants have no such protection and often live like stateless persons, at the mercy of unscrupulous employers and criminal gangs, unable to find proper accommodation, without access to healthcare, and always under the threat of discovery and deportation.

While these may seem to be fairly straightforward definitions and distinctions, the reasons people "freely" leave their home are complex. It is often hard to distinguish between migrants who left their countries because of economic problems or environmental degradation and others who left because of political persecution or conflicts. Often the various reasons are interlinked, and it may be hard to distinguish between a refugee and a migrant. People leave because they feel that being able to survive and maintain their well-being is no longer possible in their home country. For example, conflict may destroy the environment, thus forcing people to move. In another context, war may have destroyed the economy of the country, and people are no longer able to earn their living and sustain their families. They then leave the country in order to survive. In both cases, it would be hard to distinguish between migrants and refugees. In either case, people have been "forced" to leave their home and country.

Regardless of which category described in this section that foreigners belong to, the UNHCR report *The Rights of Non-Citizens* identifies the challenges foreigners face.

> For non-citizens, there is, nevertheless, a large gap between the rights that international human rights law guarantees to them and the realities that they face. In many countries, there are institutional and pervasive problems confronting non-citizens. Nearly all categories of non-citizens face official and non-official discrimination. While in some countries there may be legal guarantees of equal treatment and recognition of the importance of non-citizens in achieving economic prosperity, non-citizens face hostile social and practical realities. They experience xenophobia, racism and sexism; language barriers and unfamiliar customs; lack of political representation; difficulty realizing their economic, social and cultural rights – particularly the right to work, the

> right to education and the right to health care; difficulty obtaining identity documents; and lack of means to challenge violations of their human rights effectively or to have them remedied. Some non-citizens are subjected to arbitrary and often indefinite detention. They may have been traumatized by experiences of persecution or abuse in their countries of origin, but are detained side by side with criminals in prisons, which are frequently overcrowded, unhygienic and dangerous. In addition, detained non-citizens may be denied contact with their families, access to legal assistance and the opportunity to challenge their detention. Official hostility – often expressed in national legislation – has been especially flagrant during periods of war, racial animosity and high unemployment.[19]

International Laws and Conventions Related to Displaced Persons

The twentieth century witnessed significant steps in addressing the phenomenon of displacement within legal and global frameworks. As a result of the two world wars and subsequent conflicts that resulted in massive human tolls of the numbers killed, wounded, and displaced, the international community developed laws and legal conventions to protect non-combatants who are affected by conflict and displaced, either forcibly or voluntarily.

The Geneva Conventions

The Geneva Conventions are four treaties and three additional protocols that are international laws created to ensure the protection of civilians during armed conflict. The original treaty was adopted in 1864, and the fourth version became part of international law in 1949. Three other treaties together with the latest version of the 1864 treaty became known as the Geneva Conventions. Three additional protocols to the conventions were added in 1977 and 2005. The first treaty of 1864 led to the establishment of the Red Cross in Geneva.

The Geneva Conventions are meant to protect those who are not part of an armed conflict. Besides civilians and humanitarian aid workers, they also protect wounded soldiers and prisoners of war.

19. UNHCR, *Rights of Non-Citizens*, 5–6.

	Movement beyond border?	Displaced by force or by choice?	Protected by international law?	Able or willing to live in home country?	Claim official nationality? Recognized citizens of a nation-state?	Global number estimates
Refugee	Yes	Force	Yes	No	Yes	44 million
IDP	No	Force	No	Yes	Yes	21.3 million
Stateless	Primarily No	Force	No	Yes	No	10 million
Migrant	Yes	Choice	Yes and No	Yes and No	Yes	244 million

Table 2.1. The Displaced by Categories

The Universal Declaration of Human Rights

The Universal Declaration of Human Rights (UDHR) was adopted by the United Nations General Assembly on 10 December 1948. Because of the atrocities of World War II, people felt the need for legal instruments that would protect the rights of individuals. The UDHR consists of thirty articles, which have since been elaborated in subsequent international treaties. It protects individuals from discrimination, slavery, and torture, while ensuring that everyone has the rights to maintain their well-being via access to healthcare, food, and social services. The UDHR also ensures the right to a nationality, asylum, freedom of movement, and protection from arbitrary detention.

Though they have proven to be tremendous steps forward in protecting life and advancing human dignity, international human rights agreements have not provided a durable solution to the world's enduring problems. Harvard University anthropologist and physician Paul Farmer and the author of *Pathologies of Power* provides a caution on the applicability of the UDHR. He writes, "Rights declarations are . . . exhortatory and largely unenforceable. And the bad news is that very few enjoy these rights." He further states that the struggles for social and economic rights are the "neglected step children of the human rights movement." Nigerian lawyer and human rights activist

Chidi Anselm Odinkalu writes that the needs are so serious and overwhelming that the existence and awareness of laws on human rights are not enough. "In Africa, the realization of human rights is a very serious business indeed. In many cases it is a life or death matter. . . . Knowledge of the contents of the Universal Declaration will hardly advance their condition."

The UDHR provides an important legal framework by defining what it means for an individual to live with dignity and in freedom. However, refugees, the stateless, and migrants are among the most vulnerable, poor, and marginalized in many communities. Because of this, they are unable to experience the freedom and dignity that the UDHR outlines for them. It is increasingly recognized that poverty is not due merely to the lack of access to services, but is due to the lack of human rights – more specifically, society not acknowledging the human rights of the poor, the refugees, the stateless, and the migrants. This lack of social and political justice is considered one of the key underlying causes of poverty. Jacob Kirkeman Boesen and Tomas Martin at the Danish Institute for Human Rights write, "[A Rights Based Approach (RBA) to addressing poverty] is able to recognize poverty as injustice and include marginalization, discrimination, and exploitation as central causes of poverty." In a rights-based approach, instead of being viewed as victims dependent on handouts and charity, people are viewed as having the right to meet their basic needs.

Convention Relating to the Status of Refugees

"The Convention and Protocol Relating to the Status of Refugees," also known as the 1951 Refugee Convention, builds on article 14 of the UDHR to ensure protection of individuals fleeing from persecution or violence targeted at them in their home country. It clearly defines who is a refugee and who is not, though there is some room for interpretation. A critical part of the convention and the protection of individuals under threat is the principle of *non-refoulement.*

> No Contracting State shall expel or return ('refouler') a refugee in any manner whatsoever to the frontiers of territories where his life or freedom would be threatened on account of his race, religion, nationality, membership of a particular social group or political opinion." (Article 33:1)

Once granted refugee status, individuals cannot be returned to their home country where they faced threat.

Guiding Principles on Internal Displacement

In 1993 Francis Deng, representative of the UN secretary general at the Commission on Human Rights, prepared the first study of international standards relevant to IDPs. This study was then presented in 1998 to the Commission on Human Rights of the United Nations as the "Guiding Principles on Internal Displacement." Like the 1951 Refugee Convention, it outlines protections for those who have been forcibly displaced from their home but have not crossed an international border and remain in their own country.

International Convention on the Protection of the Rights of All Migrant Workers and Members of Their Families

"The International Convention on the Protection of the Rights of All Migrant Workers and Members of Their Families" was signed in 1990 and came into effect in 2003 when at least twenty countries had ratified it. In 2015, there were 244 million international migrants, an increase of 41 percent of the number in 2000. These migrants make up 3.3 percent of the global population.

This convention aims to protect the rights of all migrants (international and domestic) and their families by guaranteeing them equality of treatment and same working conditions as nationals. While legal migrants have more rights, illegal migrants also have fundamental human rights like all human beings.

1954 Convention Relating to the Status of Stateless Persons and 1961 Convention on the Reduction of Statelessness

The twentieth century produced two conventions that serve as primary guides in efforts to protect stateless individuals and eliminate statelessness: the "Convention Relating to the Status of Stateless Persons" of 1954 and the "Convention on the Reduction of Statelessness" of 1961. The former treaty addresses the treatment of stateless persons by emphasizing the "immediate need to improve the legal status and secure the . . . basic rights for the existing stateless populations around the globe." The latter presents the principles for the "reduction and indeed eradication of statelessness itself." More than a half century on, these conventions remain the most comprehensive and current global frameworks for addressing statelessness and marginalization of the stateless. However, the conventions have a regrettably low number of signatory states; only sixty-seven countries have ratified the 1961 convention while the 1954 convention has a slightly more respectable eighty-nine countries.

Conclusion: Key Issues Affecting the Displaced and Those Providing Them Assistance

Problems related to refugees, migrants, and statelessness are not localized nor limited to specific regions of the world but are rapidly growing crises in an increasingly globalized world. The plight of refugees and migrants does not simply lead to a neighbouring country. The availability of modern travel means individuals can move to any country on any continent that provides hope for starting a new life. Some of the emerging challenges in ministering to those who have been displaced and suffer non-belonging include the following:

- The sheer number of displaced in the world today is putting severe financial strains on governments and organizations that are trying to provide assistance. The shortage of funds limits how many can be helped and the type of assistance that can be administered. This means that large numbers of the displaced live in poverty on the margins of society. They are viewed with suspicion and are often considered as parasites to society and the national and international welfare systems.
- The fear of terrorism and the influx of refugees are now intertwined. Refugees are widely viewed with hostility as many suspect that some refugees might in fact be terrorists. This hostility is compounded by the fact that many refugees are culturally, ethnically, and religiously different than their host countries, which causes many in the host nations to experience discomfort and suspicion. This phenomenon is not new nor connected only with Muslim refugees and migrants. Historically, Jewish, Irish, Italian, German, Japanese, and Chinese migrants and refugees have been discriminated against in North America. More recently, Eastern European and North African migrants often face discrimination in Western Europe.
- Over the past thirty years or so, humanitarian assistance has primarily been provided by secular organizations such as the United Nations, the Red Cross, and secular NGOs. However, more and more Christian organizations and churches (as well as Islamic NGOs)

are becoming involved in helping refugees. This raises a new set of challenges as the humanitarian aid community wonders about the motives of the Christian organizations and institutions involved.

- The aid community has not always viewed faith and religion with suspicion. In the post-World War II years, according to a 1953 study, 90 percent of all post-war relief was provided by religiously affiliated agencies. However in the decades that followed, the religious motivations for providing humanitarian aid were replaced by a secular worldview, as religion has come to be seen as a hindrance to progress. The suspicion (sometimes overtly stated) is that local religious institutions are not able to adhere to the humanitarian principles of impartiality and non-conditionality.
- The first five principles of "The Code of Conduct for the International Red Cross and Red Crescent Movement and NGOs in Disaster Relief" articulate the fundamental assumptions that humanitarian assistance be non-political and impartial in terms of religion, creed, race, and nationality. The emphasis is that aid be given unconditionally and be based only on need. The only motivation for the assistance should be the humanitarian imperative. Yet this assistance needs to be balanced with a respect for local culture and customs, which invariably include religion, religious values and worldviews, and religious institutions in society.
- Some churches and mission agencies see refugees as the "new" mission field that needs to be evangelized.
- Growing religious dimensions to why people flee their homes can make the engagement of faith communities with the displaced rather delicate. These dimensions impact the assistance and protection provided to the displaced as well as the policies and social attitudes that confront them in their host countries. In the past few years (as at other times in history), many people have been driven from their homes because of their religion. While religious wars and persecution are not new phenomenon, how we respond in the light of international standards such as the Red Cross code of conduct may need to be changed to ensure that the religious dimensions of the context do not hinder providing aid.

Questions for Reflection and Discussion

1. How many of the foreigners in your community are migrants, refugees, or stateless? From what you have learned in this chapter, are you able to distinguish the different categories they fit into?
2. Identify one foreigner you know (or find someone, if you don't know any) and ask him or her to tell you their story. You might ask why did they leave their home? When did they move from their country? What was their journey like getting to their new country? What have they liked about their new country, and what have they found difficult or challenging about their new country? What do they miss about their home and their life in their old country?
3. What organizations in your community are helping migrants, refugees, and the stateless? What kind of services do they provide?

3

Biblical Foundations 1: Belonging, Displacement, and the Foreigner in the Old Testament

Israel's religion was a religion of salvation, not of contemplation – that is what accounts for the mantra of the widows, the orphans, the aliens, and the poor. Not a religion of salvation from this earthly existence but a religion of salvation from injustice in this earthly existence.

Nicholas Wolterstroff, professor of philosophical theology, Yale University[1]

When fighting erupted in Kormaganza, Blue Nile state, Sudan in September last year, eighty-year-old Dawa Musa's family decided to flee to the neighbouring village of Mafot. Dawa was too frail to make the two-day journey by foot, so her son, Awad Kutuk Tungud, hid her in the bush for three days while he moved his wife, Alahia, and nine children to safety. Awad returned for his mother and carried her to Mafot, where the family remained in relative safety for several months – until artillery began shelling the village.

Awad again fled with his family – this time across the border to South Sudan. For fifteen grueling days, he carried both his elderly mother and his daughter

1. Nicholas Wolterstorff, *Justice: Rights and Wrongs* (Princeton, NJ: Princeton University Press, 2008), 115.

Zainab on his back, until they reached the border crossing at Al Fudj in February. UNHCR transported the family to Jamam refugee camp in South Sudan's Upper Nile state. They lived in safety for seven months until heavy rains caused flooding, making it difficult for UNHCR to bring clean water to the camp and bringing the threat of highly contagious waterborne diseases.

UNHCR set up a new camp in Gendrassa, located fifty-five kilometers from Jamam and on higher ground, and began the relocation of 56,000 people to the new camp. Among them were Awad and his family. Awad carried his mother once again, but this time it was to their new tent in Gendrassa camp. Awad has plans to begin farming. "Come back in three months," he said, "and there will be maize growing."[2]

The problems of refugees and displacement cannot only be analyzed through political and social lenses. A theological and biblical framework for understanding the problems considers the reality of the fallen world we live in. Sin is not only an individual reality but is manifested in social institutions and values. American theologian Reinhold Niebuhr states that evil is often thought of as an individual trait, whereas institutions may in effect represent a far more insidious evil that is more likely to abuse power and prove usually more resistant to change.[3]

There are social, legal, and economic structures in societies that are unjust and inherently evil. These may exist in the form of deeply imbedded social attitudes, legal and economic systems, or religious and social practices that discriminate against specific peoples, groups, and individuals. Racism, apartheid, communalism, sexual exploitation, political oppression, hyper patriotism, human trafficking, forced displacement, and ethnic cleansing are just some examples of how these socially imbedded attitudes surface in everyday life, mostly with tragic results. Often these attitudes are institutionalized through laws, economic policies, and institutions that discriminate against particular groups or favour the wealthy, the elite, and specific social groups.[4]

---

2. UNHCR. "Awad's Story, South Sudan," UNHCR Stories, http://stories.unhcr.org/awad-2-p131.html.

3. Reinhold Niebuhr, *Moral Man and Immoral Society: A Study of Ethics and Politics* (New York: Scribner, 1932).

4. Others who have written extensively about institutionalized evil (sin) include Walter Wink, *Engaging the Powers: Discernment and Resistance in a World of Domination* (Minneapolis, MN: Fortress, 1992) and Walter Rauschenbusch, *A Theology for the Social Gospel* (New York: MacMillan, 1917).

These societies are the context within which displacement, with its devastating consequences of dehumanizing individuals and whole communities, takes place. It also highlights our role as a society in any refugee or migrant crisis and how displaced people are treated. This is also the context within which God responds and brings healing and wholeness.

The central paradigm for understanding who the foreigner is in the Old Testament is the concept of belonging. Those who do not belong own no land, and as a result have no physical or social security. This concern over not belonging is an ongoing theme throughout Scripture.

The Grace and Compassion of God

Any study of the horrors of displacement has to start with understanding the nature and character of God. Displacement has always been a reality of the human experience. Because of their disobedience, Adam and Eve were displaced from the home God had created for them. Cain was judged for his jealousy and violence and driven from the area where he had made his home. Centuries later, the southern kingdom of Judah was conquered, and the elite were carried into exile because of idolatry and social injustice.

Yet what is remarkable in each instance is the character of God, who extends grace and unmerited favour to those who have been displaced, enabling them to cope with the consequences of their own actions, even though the crisis was their fault. In the case of Adam and Eve, God provided clothing so they could cope with the consequences of shame. Even in their exile from his presence, God never abandoned them but blessed them with children (Gen 4:1) and enabled them to worship him (Gen 4:3–4). God gave Cain a physical mark so that as he wandered, he would be protected and not harmed; despite the hideousness of Cain's actions, God alleviated his fears and addressed his vulnerability. God never abandoned the Israelites in exile and promised that they would be restored at the right time (Jer 29:10–14). He even instructed them on what to do so that he could bless them in exile (Jer 29:4–8), thus helping to transform their displacement from an episode of apparent hopelessness to a season of refinement and growth.

Other stories are similar. When Hagar and Ishmael were sent out from Abraham's family and tribe, God saw their desperation, nourished them, and promised them a future. When the tribes of Jacob were humiliated and enslaved in Egypt for four hundred years, away from the land they had been promised, God heard their cry and sent them a liberator. As they wandered in the desert homeless, God provided for their daily physical needs. When Naomi became a widowed migrant in a foreign land, God gave her a non-Israelite, Ruth, as her companion who then became her only family. God in his love then brought the two back to Naomi's ancestral home and gave them a home and family.

So whether people are displaced because of their own actions, are victims of the brutality of others, or are migrants in trouble in a foreign land, God is concerned for their plight and well-being. God never abandons his creation and in his righteousness will fulfil his obligation to them. God's character demonstrated through his grace, compassion, and righteousness is the starting point in knowing how God relates to refugees and the displaced.

The Foreigner in the Old Testament

The formation of Israel as a society and as a nation occurred during the exodus from Egypt and the subsequent wilderness wanderings. It was during this period through the giving of the law that Israel's social contract was developed. The Torah, or the Pentateuch,[5] weaves the narrative of Israel's story with the principles and laws that together were to form the basis of society and social discourse. During the period of the prophets, the laws provided the lens through which the prophets critiqued society and its narrative.

The Context

According to biblical scholar Roland de Vaux, ancient Israel in the wilderness was a semi-nomadic society and was not divided into social classes.[6] Israelite society as originally structured was non-hierarchical and decentralized. Missiologist Arthur Glasser at Fuller Theological Seminary writes about the value of such a quality. "It protected the social health and economic viability of the lowest unit, not wealth, privilege, or power of any structured hierarchy. Its aim was to preserve the broadly based egalitarian self-sufficiency of each family and protect the weakest, poorest, and most threatened persons in the nation."[7]

5. The first five books of the Old Testament.

6. Roland de Vaux, *Ancient Israel: Its Life and Institutions* (London: Darton, Longman & Todd, 1965), 68.

7. Arthur F. Glasser, Charles E. Van Engen, Dean S. Gilliland, Shawn B. Redford, and Paul Hiebert, *Announcing the Kingdom: The Story of God's Mission in the Bible* (Grand Rapids, MI: Baker Academic, 2003), 117.

What is remarkable is that according to the traditional dating of Exodus, Leviticus, and Deuteronomy, at least the Covenant Code (Exod 21–23) and the Deuteronomic Code (Deut 12–26) were given during the wilderness sojourn.[8] Even though the Israelites during the wilderness wandering were a very egalitarian society with no class distinctions (among the tribes of Israel, though the population did include non-Israelites also), the law addresses issues of poverty, social vulnerability, and marginalization. It warns against class distinction and the dangers of social polarization. God in his awareness of the depth of human sinfulness and propensity for evil gifted his people with the law before they even entered the land in order to ensure protection and provision for the weak, the poor, and those who live on the margins of society.

As Israel moved from the wilderness to conquest and settlement, Joshua instituted the land tenure system. The objective of these laws was to prevent any sort of absentee landlord system where a wealthy landlord would claim a percentage of the produce from land being worked by tenant farmers. Instead land ownership and use was to be based on the kinship system, which ensured the economic viability of all the Israelites.[9] All enjoyed more or less a similar standard of living with wealth coming from the produce of the land. The ideal that God intended for his people was:

"There need be no poor among you, for in the land the LORD your God is giving you to possess as your inheritance, he will richly bless you, if only you fully obey the LORD your God and are careful to follow all these commands I am giving you today" (Deut 15:4, 5).

But knowing the reality of sin and greed and its consequences, God stated: "There will always be poor people in the land" (Deut 15:11a). This was a statement of fact and of reality rather than of God's intention for his people. So he added, "Therefore I command you to be openhanded towards your fellow Israelites who are poor and needy in your land" (Deut 15:11b).

Non-possession of land during this period would be the major cause of poverty and vulnerability in society. These vulnerable members were identified as the slaves, widows, fatherless children, the needy, non-Israelites who had placed themselves under Israel's protection (from the days when they were still

8. There is considerable debate about when the various laws and codes were written and by whom. For a more detailed discussion on the dating of the various books and sections, see Harold V. Bennett, *Injustice Made Legal: Deuteronomic Law and the Plight of Widows, Strangers and Orphans in Ancient Israel* (Grand Rapids, MI: Eerdmans, 2002), 6–21. Also see Douglas A. Knight, *Law, Power, and Justice in Ancient Israel* (Louisville, KY: Westminster John Knox, 2011), 261.

9. Glasser et al, *Announcing the Kingdom*, 117.

in the wilderness), and the sojourners or "resident aliens." Therefore while the laws ensured that the vulnerable were taken care of, fundamental to everything else was to be the equitable distribution of the land and following the system (the Sabbatical and Jubilee years) that would ensure that equity and justice would continue and that generational poverty would not be perpetuated.

Foreigners in the Land

It is within this social context that the status and plight of the foreigners in ancient Israel needs to be understood. Old Testament scholar Christopher Wright identifies the various kinds of foreigners who lived in the land.

- *Gēr* (plural *gērîm*) were not ethnic Israelites but were the sojourners, resident aliens, or foreigners.[10] While they were resident in the land, some were members of an Israelite household as slaves, others were not. Those who were not slaves would not have been allowed to own land (since they were not Israelites), but many of them would have been employed to work on the land. They were not slaves, but they were on their own and vulnerable to exploitation. Most were also economically poor and all were socially vulnerable as they did not have the security of land ownership nor were they part of the Israelite tribal system.[11]

  The concept is similar to the practice among ancient Arab nomads, where a *jar* was a refugee or individual who had settled in a tribe other than his own while seeking protection. Similarly, the *ger* "is essentially a foreigner who lives more or less permanently in the midst of another community, where he is accepted and enjoys certain rights."[12] Abraham and Moses in the early years were *gērîm*. Later when the Israelites settled in the land and saw themselves as "the people of the land" and the legitimate owners, all the former inhabitants became *gērîm*, unless they became slaves or were assimilated into Israelite society through marriage. So while the *gērîm* were free men and not slaves, they did not have full civic or political rights.[13]

---

10. Lev 19:10; 23:22; Num 35:15; Deut 24:19–21.
11. Wright, "Old Testament Perspective," 3–4.
12. de Vaux, *Ancient Israel*, 74.
13. Ibid., 75.

Wright quotes biblical law scholar Jonathan Burnside to further expand this point.

> We may understand the *ger* as a person from another tribe, city, district or country who has left his homeland and who is no longer directly related to his original setting. He is someone who lacks the customary social protection of privilege and who has, of necessity, placed himself under the jurisdiction of someone else. . . . This being so, it is sensible to suggest that the noun *ger* should be translated as "immigrant." The phrase "resident alien" is awkward and the term "sojourner" is archaic. "Immigrant" . . . adds the motif of "social conflict." It does this in three main ways. First it highlights the original circumstances of social conflict that are inevitably responsible for causing people to become immigrants in the first place. People usually become *gerim* as a result of social and political upheaval. This could be caused by war, famine, oppression, plague and other social misfortunes. Second it is consistent with the conflicts that can result when immigrants try to settle in a new environment. . . . Third, it highlights the immigrant's "outsider" status in the adopted social setting.[14]

- *Nokrīyîm* and *zārîm* were foreigners who were temporary visitors, maybe merchants travelling through the land or mercenary soldiers. They were less vulnerable than the *gērîm* and usually more independent. They were sometimes viewed with suspicion and antagonistic attitudes because they worshiped idols and could be seen as a religious threat. Yet Wright points out that some kings and prophets understood the missional opportunity that the presence of these foreigners provided. "Solomon's prayer at the dedication of the temple expressed the surprising assumption that they could be attracted to come and worship Yahweh, the God of Israel, in his temple, that Yahweh would answer their prayer, with amazing missional consequences for Yahweh's reputation worldwide (1 Kgs

14. Jonathan Burnside, *The Status and Welfare of Immigrants: The Place of the Foreigner in Biblical Law and Its Relevance to Contemporary Society* (Cambridge: Jubilee Centre, 2001), 13–14, quoted by Wright, "Old Testament Perspective," 4.

> 8:41–43). Similarly, Isaiah 56:3–7 holds out the eschatological (and equally missional) promise that foreigners would come to be accepted in God's house, and their offerings at his altar (cf. Isa. 60:10; 61:5–6)."[15]

Among the foreigners in the land, the focus of concern for social protection in ancient Israel was the *gērîm*, as they were the most vulnerable among the foreigners. However, foreigners were not included in the original understanding of who were the most vulnerable in society. Glasser identifies the widows as symbolic of those most vulnerable in the community. "Widows were regarded as helpless, needy persons, unable to protect or provide for themselves. . . . In a sense widows represent all the disenfranchised persons in society, those who are deprived of reasonable livelihood and in need of care by others."[16] Old Testament scholar Norbert Lohfink referring to the context of early Israel and the surrounding cultures writes, "The fixed word-pair 'widow and orphan' is old. Israel inherited it from its surrounding cultures as a symbolic name for those in need of help."[17]

This understanding of "widows and orphans" as symbolic of all the poor and vulnerable in the community would change to include foreigners. As Israel transitioned from a group of nomadic tribes wandering in the wilderness to a nation settled in the land they were promised, the social contract that they established through the laws underscores the importance of care for the vulnerable in society. The first giving of the law in Exodus (the Covenant Code) identified foreigners as a vulnerable group, and the foundation for how they were to be treated is described in Exodus 23:9, "Do not oppress a foreigner; you yourselves know how it feels to be foreigners, because you were foreigners in Egypt." The experience and history of the Israelites in Egypt gave them a personal and deep understanding of poverty and exclusion and should have impacted their understanding of the social contract that was defined by the Covenant Code of Exodus.[18] The Israelites by then understood the devastation that displacement causes. By the time of the second giving of the law, the Deuteronomic Code (Deut 12–26), the fixed word-pair of "widows and

15. Wright, "Old Testament Perspective," 4.

16. Glasser et al, *Announcing the Kingdom*, 87–88.

17. Norbert Lohfink, "Poverty in the Laws of the Ancient Near East and the Bible," *Theological Studies* 52, no. 1 (1991): 34.

18. J. David Pleins, *The Social Visions of the Hebrew Bible: A Theological Introduction* (Louisville, KY: Westminster John Knox, 2001), 40–42.

orphans" signifying the most vulnerable and poor[19] also included the stranger in the land (Deut 24:20). *The term* poor *whenever used in both the Old and New Testaments always includes the widows, the orphans and the resident foreigners.*

The inclusion of foreigners is significant. The texts of cultures surrounding ancient Israel, such as Egyptian wisdom texts and prayers and royal texts of other ancient Near Eastern societies, included the ideology of being just and compassionate to the poor in everyday life, in business dealings, and in the courts. But they said nothing about care for the foreigners who did not belong to the community and nation. A king's concern was only for his citizens and never the foreigners. This unique distinction of concern for vulnerable foreigners in Israel's law speaks of God's compassion for the displaced.[20]

Wright summarizes the laws that supported and protected the vulnerable foreigners in ancient Israel: (a) They were protected from general abuse and oppression (Lev 19:33). (b) They were protected from unfair treatment in court (Deut 1:16–17; 24:17–18). (c) They were included in the Sabbath rest (Deut 5:12–15). (d) They were included in worship and covenant;[21] (e) Employers were to treat foreign workers fairly, just as they treated Israelite workers (Deut 24:14–15). (f) Foreigners were given access to agricultural produce through gleaning rights (Lev 19:9–10; Deut 24:19–22). (g) Foreign slaves were to be granted the right to asylum and not forcibly returned (Deut 23:15–16). And finally, (h) Foreigners were to be treated like the native-born (Lev 19:34).[22]

The command and motivation to love the foreigner is summarized in Deuteronomy 10:17–19. "For the LORD your God is God of gods and Lord of lords, the great God, mighty and awesome, who shows no partiality and accepts no bribes. He defends the cause of the fatherless and the widow, and loves the foreigner residing among you, giving them food and clothing. And you are to love those who are foreigners, for you yourselves were foreigners in Egypt." Wright adds that the motivation to love the foreigners was Israel's

19. Lohfink, "Poverty in the Laws," 34.

20. Rupen Das, *Compassion and the Mission of God: Revealing the Hidden Kingdom* (Carlisle: Langham Global Library, 2016), 49–54; 58–62.

21. Chris Wright explains that they could partake of the Passover (if circumcised, Exod 12:45–49). They were included in the joy and holiday of the annual feasts (Deut 16:11, 14). They were to observe the Day of Atonement (Lev 16:29). They were to be present at occasions of covenant renewal and the reading of the law (Deut 29:10–13; 31:12). Wright, "Old Testament Perspective," 5.

22. Ibid., 5–7.

own history of having been vulnerable foreigners in Egypt, the character and historic actions of God, and the desire of God to continue to bless his people.[23]

Centuries later the critique of social injustice in Israel by the prophets is damning. As ancient Israel evolved as a political entity, a theocratic society based on worship of the living God who had revealed himself and governed by the Mosaic laws, the Israelites were gradually influenced by values and ethics of the surrounding nations. They forgot God's values. Jeremiah reminds the nation of what was important when he writes about the king, "He did what was right and just, so all went well with him. He defended the cause of the poor and needy, and so all went well. Is that not what it means to know me?" (Jer 22:15–16). As pagan worship, idolatry, and social disintegration took hold in Israel, God sent prophets to warn his people of impending judgment if they did not return to him. Jeremiah warns them, "If you really change your ways and your actions and deal with each other justly, if you do not oppress the foreigner, the fatherless or the widow and do not shed innocent blood in this place, and if you do not follow other gods to your own harm, then I will let you live in this place, in the land I gave your ancestors for ever and ever" (Jer 7:5–7).[24]

Finally, God delivers judgment via the Babylonian conquest and exile. His verdict is damning against his people who rejected him as the God worthy of worship and as the king to be obeyed:

- They had betrayed him and his love for them. They were unfaithful to the covenant they had with God, and they worshiped idols (Exod 32:1; Isa 5:8–24; Hos 2:1–3, 8–13; Amos 2:7–8, 10–17; 5:25–27; Mic 2:1–2).
- They were unjust in their dealings and exploited the poor and the minorities (foreigners) in their midst (Amos 2:6–7a; 5:7–12).

---

23. Ibid., 7.

24. God warned the Israelites numerous times. "This is what the LORD says: Do what is just and right. Rescue from the hand of the oppressor the one who has been robbed. Do no wrong or violence to the foreigner, the fatherless or the widow, and do not shed innocent blood in this place" (Jer 22:3). "See how each of the princes of Israel who are in you uses his power to shed blood. In you they have treated father and mother with contempt; in you they have oppressed the foreigner and mistreated the fatherless and the widow. You have despised my holy things and desecrated my Sabbaths. In you are slanderers who are bent on shedding blood" (Ezek 22:6–9). "The people of the land practice extortion and commit robbery; they oppress the poor and needy and mistreat the foreigner, denying them justice." (Ezek 22:29). "So I will come to put you on trial. I will be quick to testify against sorcerers, adulterers and perjurers, against those who defraud laborers of their wages, who oppress the widows and the fatherless, and deprive the foreigners among you of justice, but do not fear me," says the LORD Almighty" (Mal 3:5).

It is important to note that God's judgment for exploiting the poor is not just limited to Israel. God hates it when any nation abuses and exploits the poor. Ezekiel 16:49 gives an additional reason for God's judgment of Sodom: "Now this was the sin of your sister Sodom: She and her daughters were arrogant, overfed and unconcerned; they did not help the poor and needy." Professor of Old Testament at Gordon Conwell Theological Seminary Timothy Laniak explains that because human beings everywhere bear God's image and likeness, he has a stake in how humans are treated.[25]

Conclusion

When God created this world he envisaged just societies that would reflect his very nature and character. The laws he later gave to the Israelites were to be the social contract of his people, and they reflected the character of God. There is no duality in Hebrew thought; the physical world is to reflect the reality of the spiritual realm. The unseen God is to be perceived not only through the laws he gave, but also through the attitudes and practice of his people. They are to be a compassionate people because he is a compassionate God. He cares for those who are unable to enjoy the blessings of his creation and live in poverty on the margins of society – the widows, orphans, and foreigners who have no family or community to support and protect them. Such compassion and social justice is fundamental to what it means to be a people of God.

Questions for Reflection and Discussion

1. Think of the times when you feel your country or society turned away from God and did things that broke the laws of God. Then reflect on ways God has continued to pour out his love and concern for your country and society. How do you see and experience the love and goodness of God in your life and in your community?
2. How welcome are the foreigners in your community? Have they assimilated to the local culture or have they set up their own distinct communities and keep to themselves? How do you feel about the

25. Timothy S. Laniak, *Finding the Lost Images of God* (Grand Rapids, MI: Zondervan, 2010), 48.

presence of foreigners in your community? Are they a positive or negative influence?

3. Look at the foreigners in your community. What are their reasons for leaving their home and their country to live where they are living now? How do people and employers in your community treat these foreigners?

4

Biblical Foundations 2: The Foreigner and Migrant in the New Testament and the Early Church

The legitimacy of the cry of the poor created a social awareness that the powerful were obligated to provide justice and protection for the poor. Through the work of the bishops the poor were given a voice.

Walter Brueggemann, Old Testament scholar and theologian[1]

Gabriela was a university graduate in Colombia with a degree in social service.[2] *Upon graduation she started a small community organization to help the poor in urban areas improve the quality of their lives, while her husband worked as an accountant. Because of her work and influence in local communities, Gabriela became a target for FARC (Fuerzas Armadas Revolucionarias de Colombia) paramilitary groups who started harassing her. They made her an offer to stop the harassment if they could use her small family foundation as a front for money laundering and other illegal activities. She refused.*

One day Gabriela was warned through some close friends that she was going to be killed by FARC. Realizing that the threat was real, she and her husband quickly gathered their three children, their legal documents and a few precious

1. Walter Brueggemann, "How the Early Church Practiced Charity," *The Christian Century* (June 2003): 30.

2. Names and some details have been changed to protect the identity of the individuals mentioned so they may not be put at risk.

items, and fled to neighbouring Ecuador. After a few weeks in a village near the border, they realized that they were not safe there from the reach of FARC and decided to move to the capital city, Quito.

Because Gabriela and her family were in the country illegally, they could not find proper jobs nor a decent place to stay. They found a room in a shanty town in the city and paid for it with what they earned as daily manual labourers. In the three years Gabriela has been there, her family has been victims of physical violence and as a result live in constant fear. She and her daughter have often been threatened sexually. Most days they are able to earn enough to buy some bread and a little milk, and Gabriela picks up some discarded vegetables from the market nearby, enough for the only meal they have during the whole day. They are constantly hungry, and the children, who are not yet teens, are already showing physical signs of malnutrition. The children are unable to attend school and often help their parents in the manual work that they do. It is not unusual to spend a whole day working and then not be paid in the evening or be paid only a small portion of what they had been promised. There are no social services or civil society organizations in their area that they can turn to for help.

This is a far cry from the comfortable middle class existence Gabriela and her family had enjoyed in Colombia. They fear for their family members left behind and wonder if they will ever see them again. They would like to be resettled in another country, but they have been told that once they register with the UN, the waiting list is several years long and there are no guarantees. It is the daily fear and the uncertainty of the future that is the most difficult for them to cope with.

The terms *refugee*, *migrant*, and *stateless* are technical categories used to distinguish people in particular situations in our modern world. The terms are specific to the global legal realities of our contemporary context; they were not used at the time of the New Testament. Even so, the situations these terms denote were very much part of the context of the New Testament world. Significant population movements changed the demographic landscape of the Roman Empire, particularly in the cities. By the first century, Palestine was not just a stop along the trading routes but a major centre of commerce and trade, as well as a centre of political power. This change resulted in an increase in the foreigner population who arrived as slaves, labourers, artisans, soldiers, and businessmen.

The paradigm of belonging permeates the New Testament. While these foreigners included merchants, traders, and wealthy Roman officials, the majority were migrants who could be counted with the Jews of whom most were poor. Basically, the foreigners were largely unwelcome, and even despised by the Jews, regardless of whether they were rich or poor.

Jesus and the Vulnerable Foreigner

The Gospels do not directly address the phenomenon of displacement or refugees. They occasionally refer to strangers and briefly mention that Jesus as a child was a refugee when his family fled for a period to Egypt when the lives of young Jewish males were at risk. However, Jesus's teachings and actions follow in the tradition of the Old Testament in showing compassion for the vulnerable in society.[3] Caring for the poor was a matter of urgency considering at least 75–80 percent of his audience was poor, which included foreigners residing in and around Palestine.[4]

Even though Galilee was located at the crossroads of highways from Europe, Asia, Africa, and the rest of the Middle East, only a few of Jesus's encounters with foreigners are recorded. In his conversation with the Samaritan woman at the well, we see an apparently scandalous interaction with a person belonging to a community that was despised and marginalized by the Jews. Jesus transcended the mentalities of the day and showed respect, compassion, and understanding in ways that challenged religious and social status quos. When a centurion of the hated Roman occupying army approached Jesus to heal his servant, Jesus honoured the centurion in front of the crowd for his understanding of authority and faith, while granting his request to heal the servant (Luke 17:1–10). During a visit to Tyre, when a Syrian Phoenician woman approached Jesus asking him to deliver her daughter from demonic spirits, Jesus did not ignore her because she did not belong to the Jewish community. He healed her daughter (Mark 7:24–30). In each instance, Jesus

3. When Jesus spoke about the poor, he was referring to the majority who were oppressed because of the greed and injustice of a small, wealthy, and powerful elite. When he taught and preached, many of his listeners were the chronically poor and those living in extreme poverty on the fringes of society, while some from the wealthy and elite sections of society listened in. He used parables about being exploited that they could relate to (Matt 18:21–35). He spoke about a God who cared enough to feed the birds of the air and clothe the flowers of the field because these people were worried about their next meal and probably did not have a spare set of clothes or enough warm clothing for the winter (Matt 6:25–34). Jesus fed them as they listened to him teach because they did not have enough food with them (Matt 14:13–21).

4. Philip A. Harland, "The Economy of First-Century Palestine: State of the Scholarly Discussion," in *Handbook of Early Christianity: Social Science Approaches*, ed. Anthony J. Blasi, Jean Duhaime, and Philip-Andre Turcotte (Walnut Creek, CA: Alta Mira Press, 2002), 515.

showed respect to foreigners, to "outsiders," and compassionately met their needs while making no distinction between them and the poor and vulnerable Jews he ministered to.

When Jesus described the judgment seat of Christ in Matthew 25:31–46, he specifically mentioned care of strangers as a trait of the faithful ("I was a stranger, and you welcomed me." v. 35). *Strangers* in first-century Palestine were non-Jewish foreigners, and most tended to be poor people who did not belong to a community for support and protection. Jesus stressed that those strangers who were desperate and in need were as much his concern as the Jewish poor, widows, and orphans. Because these strangers were not known in the community, they could very well have been angels of God! (Heb 13:2)

While the needs and problems of the poor are different than those of people who have been forcibly displaced from their homes, both groups are vulnerable, experience deprivation, and often face discrimination. When Jesus spoke about the poor, he was referring to those who are marginalized, including the foreigner who has no support or protection in the local community. The Old Testament often referred to the poor with the word combination of "widow, orphan, and foreigner," and this conception of poverty continued in New Testament Palestine. The concept included the poor who have been robbed of their land by the manipulations and deceit of the wealthy.[5]

God's attitude towards the vulnerable (the poor, migrants, refugees, disabled, and others) is probably most clearly seen in two of Jesus's parables. The first is the story of the Good Samaritan (Luke 10:25–37). The expert in the law quotes from Leviticus 19:18 saying, "love your neighbour as yourself" (Luke 10:27). But in answer to the expert's question, "Who is my neighbour?" Jesus intentionally does not identify the religion or ethnic background of the man waylaid by the robbers. The point he was trying to make is that one should not only respond to the needs of one's family, tribe, or fellow religious adherents. The people of God are to be compassionate to anyone in need, regardless of their legal status, ethnicity, religion, social standing, or affiliation of any kind.

The second parable is about Lazarus the beggar. Jesus directly addresses the dynamic of the rich and poor in first-century Palestine where the rich were immortalized by lavish burial tombs that honoured their name and memory while the poor were disposed of in anonymity. Strangely, Jesus leaves the rich man anonymous and thus having no lasting honour. Going against the cultural

5. Das, *Compassion and the Mission of God*, 63–68.

norm, Jesus instead honours Lazarus, a man who was not only poor but also a beggar possessing no wealth or social standing. Jesus gives no indication of why Lazarus is poor or to what ethnic group he belonged, but Lazarus is remembered by history through the living memorial of the parable. By naming Lazarus, Jesus identifies him as a unique individual, not just one of the poor who hide in shame.

The name of the beggar is Lazarus, which is derived from Hebrew אלעזר, El'āzār, meaning "one whom God has helped." Through this story, Jesus reveals the heart of God for the poor and the broken. The dogs, whose saliva is healing for his sores, care for Lazarus. God's creatures have more compassion for the beggar who was sick and desperately hungry than the rich man, who was oblivious of Lazarus's existence, though he likely passed him every day as he went in and out of his house. *The rich man is not condemned for being rich, but for not being concerned for the poor.* His concern right to the end remains only for his family and never for those who were not part of his social circle. He excludes the outsider as not being worthy of his attention and care.

In both parables, Jesus highlights a deeply ingrained cultural value in the Middle East where people are concerned only for those who belonged to their community and family, to the exclusion of everybody else. Ibn Khaldun, the Tunisian Arab historian and sociologist in the fourteenth century, observed that tribes survived by taking care of their own and rarely those who belonged to other tribes.[6] Such a mentality and practice was commonplace in antiquity. Jesus, however, challenges this prevailing attitude by redefining who is worthy of compassion – not just one's own family and religious community, but anyone in need, even one's enemy!

The most remarkable thing in the second parable is that Lazarus never complains nor speaks throughout the parable. In this culture, he would not have been allowed to speak to the rich. How can one so shamefully poor and socially outcast speak with an honourable member of the community? But God breaks through this stifling cultural barrier and honours the beggar by speaking for him who has no voice.

6. Cited in Ernest Gellner, *Muslim Society* (Cambridge: Cambridge University Press, 1981), x.

The Early Church and the World of Migrants

Christianity was forged in a world of flux where the challenges of migration, displacement, and even a type of statelessness had considerable impact on shaping society.

Context

In the Greco-Roman world, Roman citizenship determined not only status but often the well-being of an individual. Political status was more important than level of wealth. The primary distinctions among the population were based on whether one was a citizen or not. Citizens had economic benefits – such as landownership and political rights.[7] A Roman citizen could be wealthy or poor, but were rarely identified as such. If some were occasionally spoken of as poor, they were viewed as citizens who were in danger of impoverishment and of coming down in the world, not as those who already lay at the bottom of society.

In times of emergency, any relief provided to the poor was based on citizenship status. Those who were citizens received benefits from the emperor or the wealthy. For example, the great grain distribution of 58 AD, enacted during a period of looming food scarcity, was restricted only to citizens.[8] While there were people in the rural areas who were poor, the majority of the poor in the cities were migrants. They were socially marginalized and enjoyed no legal or political protection. This is an ancient example of a trend seen today: *in the times of social upheaval, scarcity, and crisis, it is the displaced who are cared for the least and suffer the most.*

Interestingly, the Roman Empire had a refugee resettlement policy that allowed large numbers of non-Romans into the Empire to work on the farms, not only to meet the Romans' need for farm labourers but also to maintain peace on their borders. These people were different from those who migrated to the cities. Professor of medieval history at Kings College London Peter Heather writes,

> Up to the mid-fourth century AD, the language of refuge regularly appears in Roman sources in the context of frontier management.

7. Margaret Atkins and Robin Osborne, *Poverty in the Roman World* (Cambridge: Cambridge University Press, 2006), 5.

8. Ibid., 6.

> It is employed both of high status individuals, but also – more strikingly – of very much larger groups: certainly several tens of thousands of individuals, and sometimes apparently a hundred thousand plus-strong. The basic political economy of the Empire – powered by unmechanised agricultural production in a world of low overall population densities – meant that there was always a demand for labor, and, in the right circumstances, refugees could expect reasonable treatment. Provided that their arrival posed no military or political threat to imperial integrity, refugees would receive not only lands to cultivate on reasonable terms, but might also be settled in concentrations large enough to preserve structures of broader familial and even cultural identity.[9]

The assassination of Emperor Severus Alexander in 235 AD precipitated not only a political crisis that split the Empire into three, but also an economic collapse that reached its worst point by the end of the third century when the currency no longer had any value. This crisis was followed by the forced displacement of the Goths in 376 AD and the Battle of Adrianople (now in modern Turkey) in 378 AD, which resulted in significant suffering.

In the fourth and fifth centuries as poverty increased in the eastern provinces of the Roman Empire, the cities were unable to absorb the poor, who were mainly migrants and not citizens. Princeton historian Peter Brown writes, "The existing structures of the city and the civic model that had been associated with them collapsed under the sheer weight of a desolate human surplus, as the cities filled with persons who were palpably 'poor.' They could not be treated as citizens, neither could they be ignored."[10] It was the Christians who responded to the needs of the poor. Brown writes about these Christians, "They [lay and clerical alike] were themselves, agents of change. To put it bluntly: In a sense it was the Christian bishops who invented the poor. They rose to leadership in late Roman society by bringing the poor into ever-sharper focus."[11] Adolf von Harnack, in his monumental book *The Mission and the Expansion of Christianity*, argues that the "Gospel of Love and Charity," where

---

9. Peter Heather, "Refugees and the Roman Empire" (2015), https://podcasts.ox.ac.uk/refugees-and-roman-empire.

10. Peter Brown, *Poverty and Leadership in the Later Roman Empire*, The Menahem Stern Jerusalem Lectures (Hanover, NH: University Press of New England, 2002), 8.

11. Ibid., 8–9.

the church demonstrated the love and compassion of God by helping those in need, was the main factor in the rise of the church.[12]

Migrants

Missiologist Samuel Escobar, looking at the long list of people the apostle Paul sends greetings to in Romans 16, writes that there was significant migration in the Roman Empire in the first century when people moved from the poor and underdeveloped regions of the Empire towards Rome and the other major cities looking for jobs, security, and a future. Christians were no exception in this migration. Escobar writes that some were scattered because of religious persecution (as in Acts 11:19), while others such as Paul moved voluntarily for missionary purposes (Acts 13–14; 15:36–20:38).[13]

Escobar traces some of the individuals Paul refers to who were migrants in Rome. Aquila, the husband of Priscilla, was a Jew from the region of Pontus who had to leave Rome because of the imperial persecution of the Jews (Acts 18:1–4). He and Priscilla returned to Rome years later. In between, they were migrants who moved from place to place plying their trade, sometimes with Paul. There were a number of Jews in the church at Rome who had either migrated to Rome or whose families had at one point. These were Mary, Andronicus and Junias, Herodian, and the kinsmen of Paul. He also mentions Gentiles. These included Phoebe, Narcissus, Ampliatus, and Urbanus. The church in Rome crossed cultural and ethnic boundaries and forced the new followers of Christ to deal with attitudes of racism and discrimination. It is in this context that Paul wrote to the church in Rome to, "Accept one another, then, just as Christ accepted you, in order to bring praise to God" (Rom 15:7).[14]

The Christian Response

Church historian Wayne Meeks, writing about the economic profile of the early church in Rome, states, "the prevailing viewpoint [was] that the constituency of early Christianity . . . came from the poor and dispossessed of the Roman

---

12. Adolf von Harnack, *The Mission and Expansion of Christianity in the First Three Centuries*, trans. James Moffatt (New York: Harper and Brothers, 1962).

13. Samuel Escobar, "New Testament Theological Basis" (Oxford, 2016), 3. An unpublished paper presented at the Stott-Bedaiko Forum entitled "The Refugee Crisis: Our Common Human Condition."

14. Ibid., 3–5.

provinces,"[15] namely migrants. However, the apostle Paul also mentions by name certain fairly well-to-do Christians who possessed rooms so large that "house churches" could gather in them, though the majority in the congregation members were middle or lower class.

This diversity would explain the specific exhortations of Paul who seems to be addressing urban Jesus-follower groups who were primarily comprised of people of lower socio-economic status (the poor) and only a few of the poorest (the destitute) in the community (1 Cor 16:1–2; 1 Thess 4:11–12). He exhorts Christians to work with their hands so that they can support others in need (Eph 4:28).[16]

Meek mentions some of the factors that attracted people in Rome to the Jesus groups. These congregations were generous, offered intimacy in a social context that marginalized the majority who were not citizens, and disregarded social status, all of which were radical ideas in the social and political climate of first-century Rome.[17]

These ideas of compassion and equality are based on Paul's theology of the "body" in 1 Corinthians 12 and Romans 12, which is characterized by various individuals working together. They are not only connected to the gifts of the Holy Spirit, but also include the stronger members of the body taking care of the weaker ones. Theologian Bruce Longenecker refers to these ideas as not communism, not charity, but community.[18]

A critical question is whether the generosity was directed to the poor insiders exclusively or included those on the outside. It is generally agreed that care for the poor was primarily practiced within the Jesus groups, with members helping each other – and there are similar parallels in Jewish synagogues and Greco-Roman associations who offered aid to their members. Considering that the Jesus groups consisted primarily of the middle and lower socio-economic groups and the large numbers of poor in the urban areas, we can surmise that there were limited resources available to provide support to those within the group, leaving little for anyone outside.

While this situation may have been the reality, Paul is very clear on what the ideal should be. In Romans 12:13 he writes, "Share with the Lord's

15. Wayne A. Meeks, *The First Urban Christians: The Social World of the Apostle Paul* (New Haven, CT: Yale University Press, 1983), 51–52.

16. It was usually the poor who were involved in stealing as a means of surviving.

17. Ibid., 213.

18. Bruce Longenecker, *Remember the Poor: Paul, Poverty, and the Greco-Roman World* (Grand Rapids, MI: Eerdmans, 2010), 287.

people who are in need. Practice hospitality." In Galatians 6:10 he clarifies this statement further, "Therefore, as we have opportunity, let us do good to *all people*, especially to those who belong to the family of believers" (emphasis added). In 1 Thessalonians 5:14–15, Paul stresses the need to help the weak and "strive to do what is good for each other and for everyone else." So while the reality of the limited resources likely focused the assistance within the Jesus groups, the ultimate focus has always been beyond the group.

Conclusion

God is a gracious God who, even in the midst of evil and misfortune, shows us compassion. Scripture is very clear in both the Old and New Testaments that God is concerned for the vulnerable foreigner in the community that mirrors his concern for the poor. God designed people to belong to a community where they would not only find life but also where they would have an identity. Migration and forced displacements have been a reality throughout history. Whether in ancient Israel in the Old Testament or the church in the New Testament, the command and the encouragement is to welcome strangers as if they were part of your own family.

Questions for Reflection and Discussion

1. Are there any similarities between what happened in the Roman Empire and the world today?
2. Reflect on the example of the early church. What are some lessons that are relevant for the church today?
3. Do you think that helping refugees and migrants is part of the role and mission of the church? Why, or why not?

5

Theological Foundations: The Importance of Place and the Need to Belong

It is rootlessness and not meaninglessness that characterizes the current crisis. There can be no meanings apart from roots.

Walter Brueggemann, Old Testament scholar and theologian[1]

Arif is a Rohingya, who is now a refugee in Bangladesh.[2] *He cannot recall when his family moved from their native Bangladesh to Burma. All he remembers is that his father and grandfather had always been in Burma, and he grew up in a small village in northwest Burma. It had always been home for him. Though he is a Muslim, he never thought of himself as anything but Burmese. His family lived in the village, and he had a small plot of land which he farmed. His family had some cows and bulls, and a herd of goats. What Arif and hundreds of thousands of Rohingya in Burma do not have, however, is nationality. They are stateless.*

Some years ago Arif was recruited into the Burmese army. Instead of being a soldier, he was made to work carrying supplies through the jungle, often without food and water and in slave like conditions. Because his children were still small at the time, his family was unable to cope with their small farm. Without an adult male in the house, people started stealing their cattle, and the fields began to be neglected. The hardest part was when people in the village and the

1. Walter Brueggemann, *The Land: Place as Gift, Promise, and Challenge in Biblical Faith*, 2nd ed. (Minneapolis, MN: Augsburg Fortress, 2002), 4.

2. The names and some of the details have been changed to protect the identity of the individuals so they may not be put at risk.

neighbouring town would shout abuses at them and tell them to get out since they were foreigners and not "real" Burmese.

Finally, Arif deserted from the army, gathered his family, and fled to Bangladesh. They walked for three days through the jungle until they reached a refugee camp in Bangladesh. That was fifteen years ago. Life in the camp is hard as the family can not find much work to do. One day, their teenage daughter was raped, and the authorities did nothing to find the perpetrator.

Being ethnically Rohingya, Arif and his family were denied Burmese citizenship. As refugees in Bangladesh, they are not entitled to Bangladeshi citizenship. They have no home and nowhere to go as they don't have any travel documents.

Because of recent publicity of the plight of the Rohingya refugees, one of the UN agencies is working to try to resettle them in a third country. After all these years, Arif and his family hope they can rebuild their lives in another country. But they still dream of their home and little farm in Burma and wonder if they will ever be able to go back, because that was home for them.

The biblical narrative is rich with insights about people on the move. It tells the stories of individuals and entire nations who either flee from evil, are sent into exile, wander lost, or migrate to seek a better life. When they finally find a home and are settled in a place, they experience the peace and security of belonging.

Too often church ministries to refugees, migrants, and the stateless focus exclusively on addressing physical needs and cultural orientation – including housing, jobs, access to health care, food, schooling for children, language classes, and learning about the local culture. These are all critical for survival and should be part of a first response. But after these needs are met, many refugees and migrants still feel lost and unloved, as if they do not belong. This feeling is not due to ingratitude or a sense of entitlement for more. What displaced people need more than anything else is community and a place to belong. A refugee being helped by a church in Vienna, Austria, said, "When I left my home country, I lost all my friends and family. And now in this church, I have discovered a new family."

Walter Brueggemann explains that physical places have meaning in the biblical narrative. He writes, "Land is never simply physical dirt but is always physical dirt freighted with social meanings derived from historical experience."[3] Physical land in a specific place with all the familiar sights, sounds, smells, and memories is where people have their sense of belonging. It is this specific land which gives them life as they grow their own food or earn their living, where they raise their family and make their home, and where they set up places to worship and encounter spiritual reality. Brueggemann looks at the Old Testament narrative through the lens of land and suggests that the central problem in the Bible is about homelessness (*anomie*).[4] The New Testament affirms this narrative in the letter to the Hebrews which refers to certain Old Testament characters as "being strangers and exiles" and "seeking a homeland" (Heb 11:13–14 ESV). God responds to the problem of displacement and lack of home by bringing them into an eternal city, a new home, and a new identity in a heavenly country (v. 16), a kingdom which will last into eternity.

The apostle Peter uses this imagery when he urges the followers of Christ, "as foreigners and exiles, to abstain from sinful desires, which wage war against your soul" (1 Pet 2:11). As citizens of a new kingdom, we are no longer to dwell on what has been familiar to us – the sinful desires and passions that are in conflict with the values of God – but become strangers and exiles to the lifestyle we once knew. Hebrews 12:1–2 encourages Christians to follow the example of Jesus who bore the loss of everything so that he could be "home" at the right hand of the Father. The apostle Paul writing to the church in Philippi states, "Our citizenship is in heaven" (Phil 3:20).

While much has been written on why God cares for the poor,[5] there is very little on *why God cares for the displaced and the vulnerable foreigner* (other than the fact that he simply does). God's concern for the displaced (the refugee, the stateless, and the migrant) proceeds from the simple truth that all people are created to belong to specific places, to have a home, and to belong. The apostle Paul in Athens said, "From one man [God] made all the nations, that they should inhabit the whole earth; and he marked out their appointed times in history and the boundaries of their lands" (Acts 17:26). While Paul talks about groups of people (the nations), the principle of belonging to a specific place at a specific time is just as valid for individuals. This theological dimension

3. Brueggemann, *Land*, 2.

4. Ibid., 187. Dictionary.com defines *anomie* as "a state or condition of individuals or society characterized by a breakdown or absence of social norms and values, as in the case of uprooted people." Merriam-Webster dictionary defines it as "social instability resulting from a breakdown of standards and values; *also*: personal unrest, alienation, and uncertainty that comes from a lack of purpose or ideals."

5. Das, *Compassion and the Mission of God*.

of the interaction between place and human beings needs to be understood. Philosopher and Christian mystic Simone Weil explains,

> To be rooted is perhaps the most important need of the human soul. It is the hardest to define. A human being has roots by virtue of his real, active, and natural participation in the life of the community, which preserves in living shape certain particular treasures of the past and certain particular expectations of the future. . . . It is necessary for him to draw well-nigh the whole of his moral, intellectual, and spiritual life by way of the environment of which he form[s] a natural part.[6]

The Bible consistently affirms that having social and psychological roots in this world is a significant human need and that God is concerned that people experience rootedness. This biblical concept and its implications on displacement are revealed within a theology of place.

Displacement and a Theology of Place

The biblical narrative of being displaced and then finding a home is still being played out today. What the displaced need more than anything else are people and a place; an embracing community that fosters belonging and a place that provides security. These are by no means unique needs only for those suffering displacement but rather basic human needs of all people. The Bible throughout shows that one of a person's greatest needs is to belong to a place. The tragedy of displacement is that it denies a sense of place in this world.

Place is a central aspect of the human experience. Where we are is directly tied to who we are and impacts the dynamics of our relationships at all levels. New Testament scholar Gary Burge writes, "Each of us wants a place that we can call home, a place we may think of as our own, where familiar things are available, where old stories may be retold, where we experience connection with a legacy that stretches out behind us."[7] South African theologian Craig Bartholomew calls this human need for place *implacement*, the idea that existence itself is tied to having a place.[8] He writes that God "intends for

---

6. Simone Weil, *The Need for Roots* (New York: G. P. Putnam's Sons, 1952), 43.

7. Gary Burge, *Jesus and the Land: The New Testament Challenge to "Holy Land" Theology* (Grand Rapids, MI: Baker Academic, 2010), ix.

8. Craig G. Bartholomew, *Where Mortals Dwell: A Christian View of Place for Today* (Grand Rapids, MI: Baker Academic, 2011), Kindle Location 174.

humans to be at home, to indwell, in their places; place and implacement is a gift and provides the possibility for imagining God in his creation."[9] Belonging to a place gives a person an identity. In many cultures, a person's full name will include either the name of their ancestral home or the town or village in which their family has roots.[10] The crisis of displacement matters to God precisely because belonging to a place is important to people.

The plight of many displaced is more than a problem of emotions but also a matter of law since they possess no official claim to rightfully be where they are. Achieving legal status in the places they reside can be elusive and leave individuals in precarious states of legal limbo. This problem is often compounded by the persisting trauma of having been uprooted in violent ways, often fleeing horrors and confronting threats to their lives. Stateless individuals who are denied citizenship anywhere in this world constantly feel like outsiders wherever they are, like unwanted occupiers of another's turf. Displacement is also particularly devastating for children. Their emotional, social, and spiritual growth is deeply affected by the instability they pass through, and the wounds may require a lifetime to heal. Jenny McGill writes about the impact of being displaced and dislocated.

> The migratory experience away from what is familiar brings a valuable sense of disjointedness. This feeling of dislocation positions one to recognize one's humanness and reminds the sojourner how easily one can become helpless. Without one's usual social and physical support, one is jolted from what is normally taken as a given, and the process of migration affords an opportunity to experience change and loss. Far from glamorizing the migrant's journey, these losses can be excruciatingly painful and life-threatening.[11]

Anglican theologian John Inge argues that the Bible consistently demonstrates two theological principles concerning place: "first, that place

9. Ibid., Kindle Location 698.

10. We can see this naming plainly in the New Testament. The identities of Paul of Tarsus and Joseph of Arimathea indicated not only their hometown, but also identify who they are in terms of their family, social standing, and culture. Even the Son of God is referred to as Jesus of Nazareth. After identifying that Jesus was from Nazareth, Nathaniel responds to Philip, "Nazareth! Can anything good come from there?" (John 1:46).

11. McGill, *Religious Identity*, 193.

is a fundamental category of human experience, and that, second, there is a threefold relationship between God, his people, and place."[12]

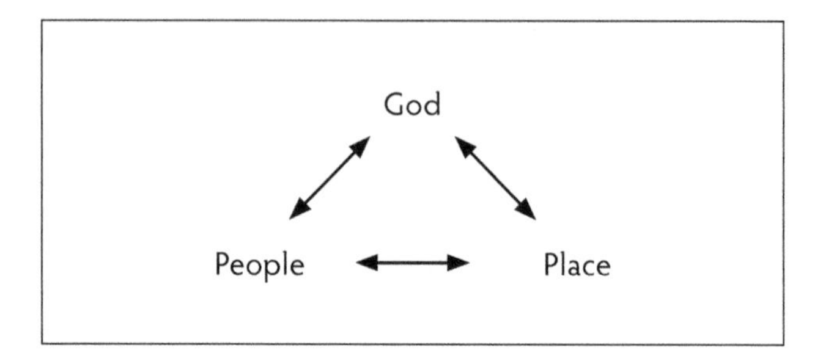

Inge states that a general problem with modernity is the "notion that place is not integral to our experience of God or the world, but simply exists alongside us as an added extra."[13]

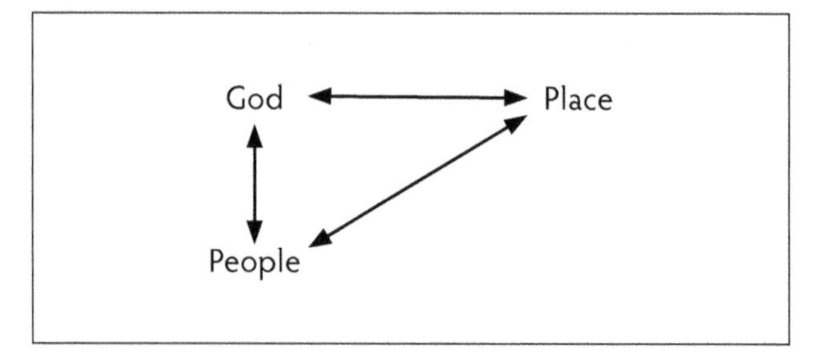

Unfortunately, this distortion of the God, people, and land relational dynamic impedes our understanding of and our responses to the needs of refugees, migrants, and the stateless. Failing to recognize the spiritual impact that occurs when place is lost limits the ability to meaningfully minister to refugees. The displaced have suffered more than simply the loss of home, lifestyle, and community; they have lost an important component to knowing and relating to God.

It is important to clarify that the issue at hand is not space, since all displaced people can make some claim to a degree of space. Rather the problem is about place. Brueggemann writes, "Land is never simply physical dirt but is always physical dirt freighted with social meanings derived from historical experience."[14] The displaced are therefore separated from their places of

12. John Inge, *A Christian Theology of Place* (Burlington, VT: Ashgate, 2003), 46.

13. Ibid., 47.

14. Brueggemann, *Land,* 2.

"historical meaning." Instead of meaningful places, they have been subjected to spaces that are uncomfortable and often oppressive. While the image of the "suffering migrant" is not always accurate – migrants, refugees, and stateless persons do achieve relatively stable situations of protection and opportunity – many others find themselves in refugee camps, urban slums, or detention facilities where life becomes an ongoing fight for survival with little sense of belonging.

Brueggemann calls the sense of not belonging, "rootlessness." He writes, "It is *rootlessness* and not *meaninglessness* that characterizes the current crises. There are no meanings apart from roots."[15] While he describes rootlessness as a problem of modern society, it is especially descriptive of the reality of refugees, migrants, and the stateless. The tragedy of displacement is not that it denies space but that it denies place where roots can be established and deepened, and where life-giving identities can be formed. Facing the legal and physical perils of displacement can lead the displaced to ultimately feel as if they do not have a place in this world altogether.

Place as both a literal and symbolic concept permeates the Bible. The opening drama of Genesis presents a theology of place "in the context of a complex, dynamic understanding of creation as ordered by God," where humanity is placed within, not above, the fabric of creation.[16] All things – plants, creatures, and most of all humans – were created to fit within a dynamic arrangement so as to foster and increase life. Our world – with all of its physical, social, and cultural dimensions – is the context within which God choses to bless human beings.

Yet it is easy to see that the current state of the world is not the way it was designed to be. Sin has devastated the entirety of the created world, not just human beings. In the Genesis account, God's judgment of sin results in displacement of human beings from Eden, banishment from their home and all that was familiar. Ever since then "the challenge of implacement and the danger of displacement are a constant part of the human condition."[17] The deep human need for belonging to a place and the impact of displacement directly leads to a crisis where individuals suffer the loss of identity and a diminished sense of self, all in addition to the threats against their physical well-being. Displacement dehumanizes its victims, yet our modern world often fails to

15. Ibid., 4.

16. Bartholomew, *Where Mortals Dwell*, Kindle Location 296.

17. Ibid., Kindle Location 698.

recognize this. Brueggemann states that existentialists do not understand that there is a "human hunger for a *sense of place*."[18] Unfortunately, many of those who are responding to the displaced do not appreciate this fundamental human need.

The lives of refugees and the stateless are dominated by their loss of home and their quest to achieve secure lives for themselves and their families. This quest is complicated by the challenges of accessing legal status within our global community of nation-states. The trauma of losing what is valuable to them (such as a home community, loved ones and friends, sentimental possessions, and dreams for the future) is compounded by the lack of legal protections and access to human rights. This situation leaves the displaced rootless within the political systems of our modern world. They have become a type of sojourner, a term that Brueggemann explains must be understood beyond the technical definition of "resident alien":

> [Sojourner] means to be in a place, perhaps for an extended time, to live there and take some roots, but always to be an outsider, never belonging, always without right, title, or voice in decisions that matter. Such a one is on turf but without title to the turf, having nothing sure but trusting in words spoken that will lead to a place.[19]

Today's "displaced sojourners" face exclusion, restrictions, and mistrust while trying to forge new lives, or while simply trying to survive. Political theorist Hannah Arendt writes vividly about the massive displacement she personally experienced in Europe during the aftermath of World War II. Her observation rings eerily true to the phenomenon unfolding today: "Once they had left their homeland they remained homeless; once they had left their state they became stateless; once they had been deprived of their human rights they were rightless, the scum of the earth."[20] All too often the current rhetoric is that the displaced are scum to be avoided rather than human beings to be protected.

Interestingly, a theology of place helps explain why there are not more displaced individuals in the world. While millions have left their homes fleeing dangers and seeking the chance for life in new spaces, many millions choose not to leave. They willingly endure hardships and threats to their very

---

18. Brueggemann, *Land*, 4. Emphasis in original.

19. Ibid., 6.

20. Hannah Arendt, *Origins of Totalitarianism* (Cleveland, OH: World Publishing, 1958), 267.

lives by remaining in lands ravaged by war, poverty, human rights abuses, and insecurity. They do so because they intuitively know that life apart from their homes, places of history, and traditions and memories is not much of a life. It is not uncommon to hear, "Better to die in my own land than live in someone else's."

Amr al-Jabali lives in the Ashar neighbourhood of rebel-controlled East Aleppo. The 54-year-old is a painter and builder, and while there is plenty here which needs rebuilding and decoration, he doesn't get much paid work these days.

He does, however, brave the bombs, the price hikes, and the electricity cuts of daily life in this part of the city, described by the UN as a "humanitarian catastrophe."

But al-Jabali won't leave. "I've never left Aleppo in my life, and by the grace of God I won't ever leave," he told The New Arab.

As many as 275,000 people remain in East Aleppo. They stay out of attachment to their homes, an inability to leave safely, for political reasons and others. These are the stories of a few of those who refuse to leave.

Al-Jabali is simply too attached to Aleppo, and has lived here since he was born more than a half century ago. Despite the current hardships, he even has hope for the future.[21]

Conclusion: Citizens of a Kingdom Above All Things

Despite historic levels of effort and resources being poured into aid and humanitarian relief, the present crises of refugees, migration, and statelessness continue to swell. Is there hope for those to whom displacement is an inescapable reality? The Bible answers with a triumphant, "Yes!" God is indeed concerned with "rootage" in our current world of political entities.

Various human rights' conventions state that everyone should have a nationality and live securely in a nation-state. The displaced should be given every opportunity to not just find a *space* where they can rebuild their lives, but be encouraged to discover and create a *place* they can call home, create history, and find meaning. The humanitarian community needs to understand this and see it as the goal, whether it is achieved by refugee resettlement in a

21. Adam Lucente and Zouhir Al-Shimale, "Holding on to Aleppo: Meeting Those Refusing to Leave," *The New Arab* (9 September 2016), https://www.alaraby.co.uk/english/indepth/2016/9/9/holding-on-to-aleppo-meeting-those-refusing-to-leave.

third country, by returning refugees to their home countries, or even while remaining stranded in their first country of refuge.

God, knowing the fragility of human existence and the corruption of social and political systems, moves beyond the physical, political, and social. *His ultimate concern is for human placement within his eternal kingdom, a security that will last for eternity.* In the Old Testament, God's desire for his chosen people was to provide a preview of his kingdom to prepare the world for when it finally arrives in all its fullness. Prophetic Scripture paints a picture of a coming place where sorrows cease, pain is no more, and injustice is eliminated.[22] Jesus built on this tradition by proclaiming the arrival of God's kingdom, and what a peculiar kingdom it is. Rather than establishing a *realm*, he declared that the *reign* of God is not limited to any physical parameters. The Gospels present a world where "sacred space is no longer defined simply in terms [that are physical] . . . but wherever Jesus is present with his followers."[23]

The New Testament refers to certain Old Testament characters as "being strangers and exiles" who were "seeking a homeland" (Heb 11:13–14 ESV). It points to a new understanding of identity that is no longer tied to a specific physical location. "No longer is a geographical place a destination of religious faithfulness,"[24] nor can any form of earthly status grant a heavenly identity.

The displaced understand Brueggemann's statement that "our lives are set between expulsion and anticipation, of losing and expecting, of being uprooted and re-rooted, of being dislocated because of impertinence and being relocated in trust."[25] In many ways they epitomize the struggle of existing "between" as they suffer the most severe of our modern world's flux and threats. Yet the Bible objects to any conclusion that the tragedy of displacement be the end of anyone's story. The enduring message of Scripture is clear: True human placement cannot be found in any physical place in the world, but rather in God who calls us out into a new consciousness.[26] The ultimate hope for the displaced, and for all of us, is that "the anticipation, the promise, is of landedness, a *place* which is rooted in the word of God."[27]

The revelation of the kingdom of God causes us to rethink the very status of the displaced. By positioning the true meaning of place and belonging

---

22. Das, *Compassion and the Mission of God*, 57.
23. J. K. Riches quoted in Bartholomew, *Where Mortals Dwell*, Kindle Location 2061.
24. Burge, *Jesus and the Land*, 99.
25. Brueggemann, *Land*, 15–16.
26. Ibid., 16.
27. Inge, *Christian Theology of Place*, 37. Emphasis in original.

within the person of Christ and his kingdom rather than in any physical place, Scripture suggests that the displaced actually occupy a spiritually privileged position within the arrangement of God's kingdom. Lebanese scholar Martin Accad argues such a dynamic in his reading of 1 Peter 2:9–10: "But you are a chosen people, a royal priesthood, a holy nation, God's special possession, that you may declare the praises of him who called you out of darkness into his wonderful light. Once you were not a people, but now you are the people of God; once you had not received mercy, but now you have mercy." He writes, "In the Bible's perspective, it is the stateless first, the non-citizens, the refugees and immigrants – before those of us who are complacently 'stateful.'"[28] Drawing the displaced into firm placement within himself is indeed at the very heart of what God has done and is doing throughout his work of salvation in this world.

McGill writes that God uses migration, even forced displacement, to reshape human identity.[29] The intent of God is therefore a type of dual citizenship where people are securely established citizens of this world (with all the status, rights, and privileges it exhibits) and citizens of God's kingdom. In this dual identity an earthly sense of belonging to a particular place and a heavenly citizenship to an eternal homeland are intertwined. Unless people are able to understand and experience what it means to physically, socially, and psychologically belong here on earth, they will have a hard time understanding what it means to belong in a heavenly kingdom. At the same time, as painful and heart-wrenching as the experience of losing everything and being displaced is, the good news is that the loss of an earthly home by no means disqualifies the refugee, the migrant, and the stateless from receiving a heavenly and everlasting citizenship, if they choose to accept the gift God offers. We should not be surprised to discover that in their desperate hunger for a home, God is bringing the displaced, those rejected by this world, into his kingdom. McGill writes, "In using migration . . . God seems to teach God's people that dwelling is more about an identity of being than a location."[30]

While the narrative of displacement is often (rightfully) a narrative of pain, struggle, and misery, those who truly engage the lives of the displaced are often inspired by what they witness. In the midst of unthinkable hardships and loss, many millions are protesting against defeat and clinging to hope

---

28. Martin Accad, "'The World Is Yours!' A Brief Reflection on Citizenship and Stewardship," *The Institute of Middle East Studies* (30 July 2015), https://imeslebanon.wordpress.com/2015/07/30/the-world-is-yours-a-brief-reflection-on-citizenship-and-stewardship/.

29. McGill, *Religious Identity*, 196.

30. Ibid., 197.

for the future. Rather than giving up on life, they continue with life. They grow from adolescence to adulthood, fall in love, get married, raise families, carry on traditions, seek to forge livelihoods, and wait for the time when their fortunes will change and their human rights and dignity will be restored. Many who have engaged compassionately with the displaced find the experience transformative; they are inspired by examples of individual faith that testify to God's nourishing presence in the wilderness and hope that a promised land is to come. If viewed with spiritual eyes, one will see among the "strangers in the kingdom" countless declarations of what Inge identifies as one of Scripture's enduring messages of hope for all people:

> The ultimate importance of the material that the Christian faith declares, is something to which sacramental encounters in the church and the world point. They point towards our ultimate destiny which is to be implaced, where the nature of the places in which we will find ourselves will be a transfigured version of the places here and now.[31]

McGill in her research with migrants found that they were in "a heightened position to search for God and seek his help. The challenges of migration offer them the precarious opportunity to rely on God through dependence on others. This means the placing of trust in fellow humans while placing ultimate dependence on God."[32] While migration and displacement are destructive to individuals and families, God uses these situations to draw people into a deeper relationship with him. Joseph the patriarch, reflecting on his forced migration from his family and home and being trafficked into the humiliation and degradation of slavery, in retrospect could say with confidence to his oppressors, "You intended to harm me, but God intended it for good" (Gen 50:20).

Questions for Reflection and Discussion

1. When you think about your home, what is it about that place that gives you a sense of home? How would you feel if you were away from it – or how did you feel when your home was taken from you?

31. Inge, *Christian Theology of Place*, 141.
32. McGill, *Religious Identity*, 195.

2. The issue of identity is complex. What are the different dimensions of your identity? How do you describe/identify who you are?
3. Displaced individuals have lost or been denied so much. What are some ways you can help them create a new home and become part of a community?
4. While respecting their faith (which may be different than yours), what are some ways you can reveal what the kingdom of God is like and share with them the God you worship?

6

Missiological Foundations: Responding to Those Who Do Not Belong

God's reception of hostile humanity into divine communion is a model of how human beings should relate to the other.

Miroslav Volf, Croatian theologian[1]

It was nearly sunset when Miriam returned to her son's tent in Lebanon's Bekaa valley. She had been with her husband and a number of her children at the UNHCR offices in Zahle where they had waited for over ten hours with hundreds of other Syrians for their case to be processed. It was a difficult day in what had become a nightmare month.

Miriam had had a simple life in Syria, in a countryside spread with orchards, farms, and the homes of her large extended family. She had raised her children there and then watched her children begin to raise their children. Then the conflict erupted. For two years Miriam and her family remained in their homes, even as the area became a battleground with rockets and shelling. Schools stopped operating, movement was restricted, and life became a struggle for survival amidst siege-like conditions. Family members were killed; loved ones began to scatter.

In the spring of 2013, Miriam and her family were faced with no choice but to flee. They first moved to another part of Syria but found no protection. They were then forced to make a risky entry into Lebanon. Miriam's initial plan was

1. Miroslav Volf, *Exclusion and Embrace: A Theological Exploration of Identity, Otherness, and Reconciliation* (Nashville, TN: Abingdon, 1996), 100.

to stay near to the Syrian border, wait for the conditions to quiet down, and then return to her land. That's the only thing she wanted, to be back in the only place she and her family have ever known as home. As weeks turned into months and the fighting became a stalemate, Miriam saw the unavoidable reality that any prospects of a return were nil. That was when she went to Zahle, where other relatives had settled nearby, to formally register with the UN.

Weary from the years and exhausted from the day, Miriam sat down and showed a piece of paper that would determine her practical status and dominate her psychological state. "It's official; we are refugees," she lamented. They had spent years avoiding this situation but now found it inevitable, and the indictment was total. Miriam, a grandmother who had simply intended to live out her days on her land in the company of her family, had reached rock bottom. She had become an occupier of another person's space, an unwanted guest in a foreign land, a liability to her new country of residency, and a legal dilemma for her world. Miriam had become a refugee.

Being hospitable to the foreigner and the weary traveller is a very ancient Middle Eastern tradition which is still practiced today by many Near Eastern tribes and communities. In the days when there were no hotels and very few caravan sarais,[2] welcoming travelling strangers was one way of ensuring that they did not die of hunger and thirst or become victims of bandits.[3] This quality of graciousness also has deep roots in Scripture. Abraham showed hospitality to three strangers, who only afterwards reveal that they were God's messengers (Gen 18:2–8). In the Old Testament the *attitude* of hospitality, of caring for the foreigner, was shown in many different forms. As with Abraham, local people were to provide the foreigner travelling through the land with food, shelter, and protection (Gen 19:1–8; Job 31:32). Foreigners along with the poor were allowed to harvest the edges of the fields after they had been harvested (Lev 19:9–10; Ruth 2:2–17). Hospitality was a quality that leaders of the early church were required to have (1 Tim 3:2; Titus 1:7–8).

---

2. A sort of inn along the trade routes of the ancient world where caravans would stop for the night.

3. There was also an accepted understanding that guests would not take advantage of, abuse, or threaten their host and would not put their host into any kind of danger.

God's Concern for the Displaced and Vulnerable

Caring for those living on the margins of society, those branded as derelicts unworthy of human dignity and rights, is truly a prophetic act. It is a radical form of protest that points to another world, another reality completely contrary to the one we live in. This active compassion demonstrates what the kingdom of God is really like – where the weak, the poor, the vulnerable, the broken, the refugee, and those rejected for whatever reason are not discarded but rather valued as individual human beings who belong. It speaks about the honour and worth of each person in the economy of God. He created them; they are of great value regardless of social or economic status, legal standing, gender, nationality, or ethnicity.

Does God care that so many are trapped in poverty and others are uprooted from their homes and find themselves with no place to belong? Jürgen Moltmann gives insight when he writes about the crucified God. He refers to the Jewish rabbi Abraham Heschel's concept of the *pathos of God*.[4] This *pathos* is not what he calls "irrational human emotions" but describes how God is affected by events, human actions, and suffering in history. Moltmann writes, "He is affected by them because he is interested in his creation, his people."[5] This *pathos* is contrasted with the *apatheia* of the gods of the religions of the ancient world that Jews and early Christians encountered. *Apatheia* was their inability to feel or be influenced. It has been transformational for many Muslim refugees and migrants to discover that God is compelled by his own nature to be deeply concerned for them and troubled by their suffering. This revelation of a compassionate Lord draws them into an intimate relationship with the living God.

God by his very nature feels, and he created human beings to be like him, to be able to feel joy, a sense of satisfaction, sorrow, disappointment, and the anguish of loss. As God sees evil and sin distort his image in the poor and the displaced, and as he sees injustice inflict merciless suffering, his *pathos* turns to wrath and judgment of those who try to destroy his creation. Old Testament scholar Timothy Laniak explains that because human beings everywhere bear God's image and likeness, God has a stake in how humans are treated.[6]

---

4. *Pathos* and *apatheia* are Greek words. Heschel's discussion on the pathos of God is from *The Prophets* (New York: Harper & Row, 1962).

5. Moltmann, *Crucified God*, 270.

6. Laniak, *Finding the Lost Images*, 48.

Rather than destroy the people he created, God suffers the anguish and agony of his own judgment. When God was crucified in Christ, he experienced a level of pain, abandonment, and suffering that had previously been unknown to him, all in order to bring healing to his creation. Japanese theologian Kazoh Kitamori writes, "The Lord wants to heal our wounds, which were caused by God's wrath; this Lord suffers wounds, himself receiving his wrath. '. . . with his stripes we are healed' (Isa. 53:5). . . . A task of the 'theology of the pain of God' is to win over the theology which advocates a God who has no pain."[7] By failing to grasp the depth of God's feelings for his creation, especially human beings endowed with his own image, people too often picture a God who is Almighty but distant and uncaring.

The *pathos* of God is the compassion that motivated Jesus throughout his ministry. The apostle Matthew observing Jesus wrote, "When he saw the crowds, he had compassion on them, because they were harassed and helpless, like sheep without a shepherd" (Matt 9:36). When Jesus healed, it was because he was moved with compassion (Matt 14:14). When he taught using parables, Jesus spoke about the compassion a father felt towards his rebellious son (Luke 15:20). Sri Lankan missiologist D. Preman Niles explains that the Greek word for compassion is *splanchnizomai* and literally means, "to be moved in the inward parts." It connotes a strong physical and emotional reaction, "a gut wrenching response."[8] It is the idea of *pathos*. Niles says that the word *splanchnizomai* only occurs in the Gospels and is only used to describe Jesus's reactions. "It is used . . . to describe the attitude of Jesus to people defined as the [multitudes] and the action that ensues from that attitude."[9] Without doubt it is the way God views the displaced today.

As God views broken humanity in the forms of the poor, the displaced, the abused, the tortured, the violated, the abandoned, and those suffering from incurable ailments and disease, his gut wrenching response is to heal, comfort, and provide. He is the God "who comforts us in all our troubles" (2 Cor 1:4). In his anger and wrath, he brings justice, and one day his kingdom will be established in all its fullness. Then all that has been perverted by sin and evil will be made whole again. "And I heard a loud voice from the throne saying, 'Look! God's dwelling place is now among the people, and he will dwell with

7. Kazoh Kitamori, *Theology of the Pain of God* (Eugene, OR: Wipf & Stock, 1965), 22.

8. D. Preman Niles, *From East and West: Rethinking Christian Mission* (St Louis, MO: Chalice Press, 2004), 79.

9. Ibid.

them. They will be his people, and God himself will be with them and be their God. "He will wipe every tear from their eyes. There will be no more death" or mourning or crying or pain, for the old order of things has passed away'" (Rev 21:3–4). God is working in history to establish his kingdom. He is working through his people today to reveal what this kingdom looks like – a place of compassion for those broken by the harsh realities of life.

Hospitality and the Concern for the Foreigner

A question to ask is whether concern for the foreigner was unique to Israel's values and culture. While ancient Egyptian wisdom texts and prayers and the royal ideology of other ancient Near Eastern nations contain much that is similar on being just and compassionate to the poor (mainly widows and orphans) in everyday life, in business dealings, and in the court, only in the Old Testament is there concern for and care of the stranger. This care is fleshed out in detail in the second giving of the law in Deuteronomy, though the idea is present in the first giving of the law (the Covenant Code) in Exodus.

Prior to the giving of the law for the first time at Mt Sinai, the formulaic language identifying the poor had been the "widow and the orphan." Nobert Lohfink suggests a variety of possible historical and sociological influences for adding the "stranger,"[10] but God states his reason in the law. Exodus 3:9 and Deuteronomy 26:7 describe the treatment of the Israelites in Egypt as being oppressed. At the end of the Covenant Code in Exodus 23:9, using the same language, God states, "Do not oppress a foreigner; you yourselves know how it feels to be foreigners, because you were foreigners in Egypt." The experience and history of the Israelites would have given them a fresh and deep understanding of this new dimension of poverty and exclusion, and impacted how they defined themselves as a society.[11] Henceforth whenever the term *poor* was used, it would now mean the "widow, the orphan, *and the stranger in the land*."

It is important to note that there is a major difference between hospitality shown towards the traveller and care for the vulnerable foreigner who lived in Israel. Hospitality was only temporary, lasting as long as travellers stayed with their host.[12] This tradition was practiced by most societies and cultures in the

---

10. Lohfink, "Poverty in the Laws," 41–42.

11. Ibid., 40–42.

12. Most dictionaries define *hospitality* as welcoming and providing for *a guest*.

ancient world and was not unique to Israel. Care for the foreigner described in Exodus and Deuteronomy is compassion for vulnerable foreigners who were living in Israel and had no social support of a family or tribe to provide for and protect them. In the ancient world, care for the poor, who were mostly widows and orphans, was the responsibility of the king and the wealthy. The foreigner in their midst who was poor was of no concern for them.[13] So the requirements in the Mosaic law for the care and protection of foreigners in Israelite communities was exceptional in the ancient world.

This law for his people reveals the character of God. He identifies himself as the protector of the poor and vulnerable. In Psalm 82:3–4, God challenges the "gods" to, "Defend the weak and the fatherless; uphold the cause of the poor and the oppressed. Rescue the weak and the needy; deliver them from the hand of the wicked." The gods failed to accomplish this, and the implication is that God is the only One who can truly provide justice and deliver the poor and vulnerable.[14]

God's defence of the poor is an integral part of his character and how he identifies himself. Psalm 68:5 states, "A father to the fatherless, a defender of widows, is God in his holy dwelling." Deuteronomy 15:9 and 24:15 both state that when the poor have been taken advantage of and cry out to God against their oppressors, the oppressors will be guilty of sin.[15] The seriousness of the crime and the severity of the punishment are described by Lohfink. "The connected sanction is that whoever forces the poor to cry will be in the state of *hêt'*. Now *hêt'* is not just any sin. As [Old Testament scholar] Klaus Koch has shown, *hêt'* is a sin which can be expiated only by the death of the sinner."[16] Unlike the ancient gods who heard the cry of the poor and either blessed them or cursed them, God defends the poor and considers their oppressors to be breaking his laws. Their condemnation is clear. Deuteronomy 27:19 states,

---

13. Das, *Compassion and the Mission of God*, 49–54.

14. Frank C. Fensham, "Widows, Orphans, and the Poor in Ancient Near Eastern Legal and Wisdom Literature," in *Essential Papers on Israel and the Ancient Near East*, ed. Frederick E. Greenspahn (New York: New York University Press, 2000), 183–84.

15. Deut 15:9 "Be careful not to harbor this wicked thought: 'The seventh year, the year for canceling debts, is near,' so that you do not show ill will toward the needy among your fellow Israelites and give them nothing. They may then appeal to the Lord against you, and you will be found guilty of sin." Deut 24:15, "Pay them their wages each day before sunset, because they are poor and are counting on it. Otherwise they may cry to the LORD against you, and you will be guilty of sin."

16. Lohfink, "Poverty in the Laws," 46, citing Klaus Koch, *Theological Dictionary of the Old Testament,* ed. G. Botterweck and H. Ringgren (Grand Rapids, MI: Eerdmans, 1974), 3: 309–320, esp. 315–16.

"Cursed is anyone who withholds justice from the foreigner, the fatherless or the widow." Exodus 22:21–24 is even more explicit. "Do not mistreat or oppress a foreigner, for you were foreigners in Egypt. Do not take advantage of the widow or the fatherless. If you do and they cry out to me, I will certainly hear their cry. My anger will be aroused, and I will kill you with the sword; your wives will become widows and your children fatherless."

Japanese theologian Kasuke Koyama writes about the implications of these passages. The issue is not just about being kind to strangers; it is a reflection of the wholeness, healing, and *shalom* that God intends for his creation.

> This extraordinary thought cultivates and expands the horizon of the human soul. It is derived from a theologically informed experience of conversion (metanoia). It reveals the truth about the creation and maintenance of shalom (wholesomeness, well-being, integrity) in human community. "You shall not oppress a resident alien," a socially marginal people. This command has remained relevant throughout the history of human civilization, and it is becoming even more significant in our own day as the number of uprooted people from political and racial oppression, inhuman poverty and ethnic conflict, civil war and natural disaster has been steadily increasing.[17]

A major distinction between Israel's social contract and the legal codes of the surrounding ancient kingdoms is that responsibility for the care of the poor and the vulnerable shifted from the king and the wealthy to the community who received the Mosaic law. The commands in Exodus 22:21–24 are clearly addressed to everyone in the community and not just to the ruler and elites. The Mosaic law described how the widows, the orphans, and the foreigners were to be taken care of by the entire community and ensured that these people were entitled to justice.

However, by the time the monarchy was firmly established in Israel in the eighth century BC, right through to the New Testament, care of foreigners seems to have been on a decline, and it is not mentioned in later Greco-Roman lists of virtues. However, Jesus resurrected the idea through his teachings (Matt 25:31–46), emphasizing that hospitality towards a stranger is an integral part of what it means to follow him. The apostles writing to the young churches

17. Kosuke Koyama, "'Extended Hospitality to Strangers': A Missiology of Theologica Crucis," *International Review of Mission* 82, no. 327 (1993): 285.

command hospitality as a part of their witness as followers of Christ (Rom 12:13; 1 Tim 5:10; Titus 1:8; Heb 13:1–2; 3 John 5–8).

Koyama connects the understanding and practice of hospitality to the great commandments – of loving God and your neighbour – and what it means to live a life that is pleasing to God. Koyama writes,

> Our "extending hospitality to strangers" happens "by the mercies of God," and when this happens our life becomes a "living sacrifice," which is "holy and acceptable to God," and it is an essential part of our "spiritual worship." There is a living connection between "extending hospitality to strangers" and "loving your God and loving your neighbor" (Mark 12:28–34) of which Christ says "there is no other commandment greater than these" (Mark 12:31). And his directive to love enemies (Matt 5:44) is the ultimate of extending hospitality to strangers.[18]

Whether it is giving hospitality to a foreign traveller passing through or longer term compassion for a foreigner in their communities who have no support or protection, the people of God are to demonstrate a different standard than the surrounding cultures whose concern is only for those who belonged to their community.

Missiological Foundation

Giving hospitality and showing compassion for the foreigner is not something that only individuals do. It is also the responsibility of the church to demonstrate the love of Christ in these ways. Croatian theologian Miroslav Volf, now at Yale, introduces the concept of exclusion and embrace that emphasizes the importance of community and belonging. He writes that so many of the sins we commit against our neighbour are acts of exclusion.[19]

Volf describes exclusion as "not recognizing the other as someone who in his or her otherness belongs to the pattern of interdependence. The other then emerges as an inferior being who must either be assimilated by being made like the self or be subjugated to the self."[20] Rather than accepting the worth and uniqueness of each individual and understanding the richness of being

18. Ibid., 284.

19. Volf, *Exclusion and Embrace,* 72.

20. Ibid., 67

interdependent with each other, we either physically and socially exclude those who do not belong to our community or require them to deny who they are and conform to the image of the community. The conforming is not to the image of Christ or to the values and standards of God, but to the social expectations of the community. From the vantage point of exclusion, the foreigner, the refugee, and the migrant are seen as a threat to the values and security of the community because they are different. Volf writes that societies who exclude have a false sense of purity and "want the world cleansed of the other rather than the heart cleansed of the evil that drives people out by calling those who are clean 'unclean' and refusing to help make clean those who are unclean."[21]

By understanding how refugees and migrants are widely mistreated and excluded from society, we can see that the basis for any ministry to them is found in God's act of redemption. Volf writes, "God's reception of hostile humanity into divine communion is a model of how human beings should relate to the other."[22] He explains that in order to move from exclusion to embrace, people need moments that provide space for repentance, forgiveness, making space in oneself for the other, and healing of memory.

In a world where violence against migrants and refugees is becoming commonplace because of the perceived threat they pose, Volf states that neutrality is not an option for the people of God, because taking the side of the suffering is the prophetic and apostolic tradition of the Bible. He writes, "These people hear the groans of the suffering, take a stance, and act. . . . After all, they are called to seek and struggle for *God's* justice, not their own."[23]

In order to understand Volf's concept of social exclusion, in particular with regards to refugees, Ibn Khaldun, a fourteenth century Arab historian and sociologist, provides insight into the nature of collectivist or communal societies. He writes, "Only tribes held together by group feelings can live in the desert" since the group ensured the survival and well-being of the individual.[24] Yet this obligation in the tribal societies of the Arab world was always limited in practice to the immediate group, family, or clan and very rarely beyond it. The reason is the concept of *assabiyah*, which Ibn Khaldun says refers to group solidarity or group consciousness. *Assabiyah* is what binds society, family, tribe, religion, and nation. It gives people a sense of belonging and

21. Ibid., 74

22. Ibid., 100

23. Ibid., 219

24. Quoted in Ernest Gellner, *Muslim Society* (Cambridge: Cambridge University Press, 1981), x.

ensures the stability of institutions in the community.[25] The fear is that a loss of group cohesion as described by *assabiyah* will result in the destruction of the community. A focus on the group cohesion ensures the survival of the group but in the process excludes the outsider or other groups.

Biblical scholar Bruce Malina explains this concept further. He writes that some societies are individualists and others are collectivists. He describes individualistic societies as contexts where "individualism is characterized by internal control and identity, as well as internal responsibility and worth." On the other, he writes,

> Collectivism may be described as the belief that groups in which a person is embedded are each and singly an end in themselves. . . . In collectivistic cultures most people's social behavior is largely determined by group goals that require the pursuit of achievements, which improve the position of the group. The defining attributes of collectivistic cultures are family integrity, solidarity, and keeping the primary in-group in "good health." . . . Should a group member fall ill, the goal of an individual's healing is group well-being. Focus is on the in-group, cooperation with in-group members, maintenance of ascribed status, and group-centred values.[26]

These ideas provide a foundation for ministering to the displaced. Refugees, migrants, and stateless individuals not only need food, shelter, access to healthcare, jobs, and education for their children; more than anything else, they need to find a community in which they can belong. In the midst of their displacement, refugees have lost their community who supported them and provided them with their social, religious, cultural, and ethnic identity. As refugees they have become foreigners who do not belong in their host communities either. As Brueggemann states, the crisis is one of rootlessness; without being physically, socially, and culturally rooted, individuals cannot find life and meaning.

In this context the church needs to be an inclusive community that embrace the outsider. If the refugees, the migrants, and the stateless are to

25. Fida Mohammad, "Ibn Khaldun's Theory of Social Change: A Comparison between Hegel, Marx and Durkheim," *The American Journal of Islamic Social Sciences* 15, no. 2 (Summer 1998): 36–37.

26. Bruce J. Malina, "Collectivism in Mediterranean Culture," in *Understanding the Social World of the New Testament*, eds. Richard E. DeMaris and Dietmar Neufeld (London: Routledge, 2010), 21–23.

know and experience the living God revealed in Jesus Christ, it will be through a community of God's people who help them rediscover their identity and enable them to belong somewhere again.

Towards a Missiology of Migration: Crossing the Divide

In trying to develop foundations for a theology of migration, Daniel Groody identifies four divides that need to be crossed. The first divide to be crossed is the *problem-person divide.* This divide is one of language that places the focus on the problem of migration rather than migrating people. Labelling people as refugees, migrants, forced migrants, immigrants, undocumented, internally displaced person, and aliens categorizes them based on issues and problems. Groody quotes Roger Zetter: "Far from clarifying an identity, the label conveys, instead, an extremely complex set of values, and judgments which are far more than just definitional."[27] To cross this divide, Groody states that human beings are made in the image of God – *imago Dei.*[28] This is not just another label "but a way of speaking profoundly about human nature."[29] *Imago Dei* resets any conversation about migrants and the displaced and provides a different starting point for how those who do not belong are to be viewed. The focus is not on the problem, but on people in need, which ensures the dignity of all people.

The second divide to be crossed is the *divine-human divide,* which involves the story of the incarnation. Groody refers to Karl Barth in stating that the incarnation is the "way of the Son of God into the far country."[30] Groody writes, "God overcomes the barriers caused by sin, redraws the borders created by people who have withdrawn from God, and enters into the most remote and abandoned places of the human condition."[31] While human migration often strives for upward mobility and trying to live with dignity, the incarnation is downward mobility and the divine willingness to undergo the most horrific degrading indignities possible (Phil 2:5–11). To cross this divide, God gives himself. "This gratuitous nature of the incarnation offers a different framework for evaluating human migration and questions some of the underlying premises

27. Groody, *Crossing the Divide,* 9, quoting Roger Zetter, "Labeling Refugees: The Forming and Transforming of Bureaucratic Identity," *Journal of Refugee Studies* 4 (1991): 40.

28. Gen 1:26–27; 5:1–3; 9:6; 1 Cor 11:7; Jas 3:9.

29. Ibid., 11.

30. Ibid., 15, quoting Karl Barth, *The Doctrine of Reconciliation*, trans. G. W. Bromiley, eds. G. W. Bromiley and T. F. Torrence (New York, NY: Continuum, 2004), 157–210.

31. Groody, *Crossing the Divide*, 15.

of the debate. . . . [It] makes profound demands on those who receive [the gift of the incarnation]"[32] and challenges us to assess our response to God's gift.

The third divide to cross is the *human-human divide.* Reconciliation between human beings is at the core of crossing this divide. Groody writes about the human tendency to idolize "the state, religion or a particular ideology and use it as a force that excludes and alienates, even when it does so under the guise of obedience to a greater cause."[33] Groody concludes,

> The *missio Dei*, in which the church participates, is not just about helping the poor but about following Christ and discovering that those whom one is called to serve also have something to give. . . . Creating space is foundational to a theology of migration because it sees the *missio Dei* not first as an imposing evangelisation but as a ministry of generous hospitality, one that is mutually enriching for those who give and those who receive.[34]

The final divide to cross is the *country-kingdom divide.* Christian discipleship, while rooted in the realities of this world, needs to ultimately be grounded in citizenship in the kingdom of God. Our vision of the kingdom of God needs to take root in the realities of our daily lives and the social contexts in which we live. It should "transfigure" the way we look at and understand migrants and others who have been displaced. It "challenges people to move beyond an identity based on a narrow sense of national, racial, or psychological territoriality. It holds out instead the possibility of defining life on much more expansive spiritual terrain consistent with the kingdom of God."[35]

Groody concludes that a theology of migration and its missiological implications "illuminates the gift and demand of Christian faith in the light of the pressing social problems of the modern world, and it opens up a

---

32. Ibid., 19–20. Gustavo Gutiérrez writes, "The condition of the poor, because it is so deeply tied to inhumanity, is a radical challenge to human and Christian conscience. No one – no matter their geographical or social location, their culture or religion – can pretend that they are not gripped by it. To perceive the condition of the poor, it is necessary to see poverty in all its depth and breadth. It is a challenge that extends beyond the social field, becoming a demand to think about how we proclaim the Gospel in our day, and how we might present the themes of the Christian message in new ways. . . . The Christian is a witness to the resurrection, the definitive victory over all forms of death." Gustavo Gutiérrez, "Memory and Prophecy," in *The Option for the Poor in Christian Theology*, ed. Daniel G. Groody (Notre Dame, IN: University of Notre Dame Press, 2007), 28.

33. Groody, *Crossing the Divide,* 21.

34. Ibid., 26–27.

35. Ibid., 31.

space to bring out what is most human in a debate that often diminishes and dehumanizes those forcibly displaced."[36] A missiology of migration focuses on human beings who are in need rather than on trying to solve a problem. By emulating God who crosses seemingly impossible divides to relate to his creation that has been debased and degraded, a missiology of migration challenges us to see beyond our self-imposed boundaries and view those who are different, and sometimes threatening, as also being made in the image of God and as people to be welcomed.

Conclusion

Any missiology that addresses human displacement must be rooted in understanding God's care for all human beings, especially the poor, the vulnerable, and those who do not belong. We should not respond to human need from the goodness of our hearts but in response to God's crossing the divine-human divide so that we can experience being loved and belonging to his eternal kingdom. Because of what we experience and witness, we are able to cross our own self-imposed barriers and divides and encounter those who are different. Ministering to their needs is not only transformative for them, but also changes us. Miroslav Volf refers to this approach as an *embrace* rather than *exclusion*. Such an embrace is showing hospitality not just to a stranger passing by but to those in our communities who have been rejected and live on its margins.

Questions for Reflection and Discussion

1. The *pathos* of God is what motivates him to respond to human need. What motivates you to want to help people?
2. What are some barriers you or your church face in trying to minister to "outsiders" in your community? What could you do to overcome them?
3. What are some ways you or your church could show hospitality to the foreigners, the lonely, and the migrants in your community?

---

36. Ibid., 32.

PART II

Ministries to Refugees, Migrants and the Stateless

7

The Local Church and Other Ministries: Enabling the Displaced to Find Space and a Place

Rumors that God was present in Christian gatherings may have also attracted outsiders to investigate Christianity.

Alan Kreider, church historian on the early church[1]

Walid has spent all of his thirty-four years in Jordan.[2] *It is the country where his parents met, where he and his siblings were born, and where he grew up, attended seminary, and served in ministry. Even so, Walid is a foreigner to the only country he has ever called home. Both sides of his family are from Palestine, but their experiences took very different turns. His mother's parents fled to Jordan during the political upheaval of 1948 and were later granted Jordanian citizenship, but his father and his family went to Lebanon. Like hundreds of thousands of others, they found themselves as stateless Palestinian refugees. When the Lebanese civil war erupted in the mid-1970s, Walid's father travelled to Jordan with his Palestinian travel document issued from Lebanon and met and married his wife. The Jordanian government granted him annual residency but did not permit naturalization. Walid and his siblings were likewise denied citizenship. (Jordanian*

1. Alan Kreider, *The Patient Ferment of the Early Church: The Improbable Rise of Christianity in the Roman Empire* (Grand Rapids, MI: Baker Academic, 2016), 109.

2. The names and some of the details of the story have been changed so the individuals cannot be identified and put at risk.

law only permits men to transmit nationality to their spouses and children. It is one of twenty-seven countries in the world that discriminates against a woman's right to pass citizenship on equal terms as a man.) Instead, they were registered as Palestinian refugees from Lebanon, making Walid a foreigner in Jordan and a foreigner to this world. He has been displaced since birth due to historical tragedies that remain unresolved and contemporary legal systems that institutionalize exclusion.

As a stateless refugee, Walid has been denied privileges and rights granted to Jordanian citizens. He is not allowed to own a home or property, qualify for health insurance, access public educational services, or pursue desired career opportunities. The challenges are practical as well as psychological. Each year Walid must apply for a one-year residency permit or risk losing any legal status in his home country. And any hope of marriage and having his own family is complicated by the fact that he cannot possess citizenship nor provide it for his children.

Walid has a deep love for Christ and a desire to be a witness to his people, country, and region. But neither Jordan nor any other Arab country will allow him the prospect of receiving citizenship and enjoying the rights and privileges entitled to all people. Walid managed to receive a visitor's visa to a Western country, and he awaits the outcome of an application of asylum that may finally grant him the form of legal belonging that has eluded him his entire life, albeit to a country in which he has no personal or emotional link. Sadly, he joins a growing number of stateless persons in the West who are stuck in legal limbo with no country to truly call home.

Having looked at the biblical and theological foundations of being displaced from one's home and how God views the displaced, the question now is, "How should the local church respond to the refugees, migrants, and the stateless – those who don't belong?" The objective of this chapter is to provide examples of local churches and ministries who are responding to the needs of the displaced and to recognize both the challenges and opportunities that accompany this work.

Dudley Woodberry, who has been a missionary in Pakistan, Saudi Arabia, and Afghanistan and then became senior professor of missions at Fuller Theological Seminary, interviewed seven hundred and fifty Muslims across the world who had decided to follow Christ and who came from thirty countries and fifty ethnic groups. Woodberry then ranked the relative importance of the influences that impacted why these Muslims chose to follow Christ. The top influence was seeing how Christians live out their faith. Many spoke about the love they experienced from Christians which in turn attracted them to the love of God. Woodberry reported, "Nearly half of all Muslims who have made a shift of faith allegiance have affirmed that the love of God was a critical key in their decision."[3] They were particularly attracted to the person, the life, and teachings of Jesus and wanted to be part of fellowships where his teachings were lived out. This is no different than what attracts the poor and the displaced to Christ.[4]

Local churches and faith communities can have a significant impact on enabling the displaced to *encounter* the living God in Christ and find a *place* where they feel that they belong. How are local churches and faith organizations responding in love and enabling the displaced to find both *space* and *place*? The following presents a number of examples.

Responding to the Influx of Refugees

Many countries in Europe and the Middle East are inundated with refugees and migrants who are either trying to find a better life in a new country or fleeing from the horrors of war in their home country. In many instances, UN agencies and national governments provide assistance to the refugees,[5] which begs the question, "Is there a role for the local church in such situations?" Below are four case studies of churches and faith-based organizations located in places with many displaced persons. While these groups could have done nothing, they chose to respond to the very human needs of refugees, migrants, and stateless individuals.

Vienna, Austria: Responding to the Refugee Crisis[6]

The church in this case study was formed around fifteen years ago out of a Baptist Union outreach to students, and their mission is to be a church that

3. D. Woodberry and R. Shubin, "Why I Chose Jesus," *Mission Frontiers* (March 2001): 15, http://www.missionfrontiers.org/issue/article/muslims-tell...-why-i-chose-jesus2001.

4. Rupen Das' ongoing research on the poor and refugees and what attracts them to Christ and the Gospel. This should be published in the near future.

5. In Africa, Latin America, and Asia most refugees are taken care of in refugee camps that have been established by the UN, national governments, or other international agencies. The opportunities for local churches to be involved are largely limited.

6. We are grateful to Cesar Sotomayor and David Bunce for providing this case study.

reaches the demographics of people who are not traditionally interested in church (such as students), those who have no background with church, and those who have been burned out by past experiences of church. The church has over one hundred and fifty members and sees total Sunday worship attendance of around two hundred people in four services (conducted in Spanish, German, Farsi, and Mongolian). Once a month, the church holds a joint service when all the congregations come together for communion and worship.

This church tries to be one that is high on permission-giving and building people up to follow their passions. So they are associated with many projects that began as people felt called to start new things: an intern school, refugee outreach, and a summer camp for young adults. They are now developing a church centre that will have a co-working space, cafe, children's group, etc. which will hopefully develop further links with the community and allow others to join in on conversations (for example with millennials) where the church has not always been well represented.

How did the church start helping refugees?

The church had been working in refugee relief and integration for around fifteen years, mainly with people from Iranian and Afghan backgrounds. The church's refugee work started as a concrete response to one refugee who ended up being deported back to Vienna under the Dublin Agreement.[7] The church was asked to provide help and support to this individual, which they were glad to do. Gradually this individual started inviting friends to the church, and a regular group emerged, laying the foundation for the current refugee-specific programs.

What kind of programs and services for refugees does the church have now? How are these programs supported and staffed?

Over the years, the church has added more facets to their refugee work. They offer weekly Farsi (Iranian) language services, faith courses, German courses, first-response trauma counselling, legal accompaniment and assistance with asylum processes, integration courses, and support in building cross-cultural understanding. They also offer a weekly coffee and conversation course for women which is aimed at language development, providing a safe space for fellowship, and offering a place for integration.

---

7. The Dublin Agreement is between the member countries of the European Union and determines where a refugee can apply for asylum, depending on where they entered the European Union.

The church has one part-time employee in the refugee work who is responsible for both overseeing the social work aspect and functioning as the main pastor for the refugee group. Alongside him is a large team of volunteers who help with some of the legal advice and services implementation and who teach German courses. The church is also looking at expanding its volunteer base in the areas of theological education and catechism in order to spread this work over a broader team.

The programs are funded through a variety of grants from Baptist organizations, including the European Baptists and German Baptists. The church also relies on the donations of countless individuals. The funding is administered under the umbrella of the local Baptist aid organization, which allows the church some legal advantages in terms of VAT taxation and tax-deductible donations. Finances are one of the biggest bottlenecks of the church's refugee work. While it is amazing to see what God has provided and how generous people are, financial constraints prevent the church from offering the services they would like in some instances. For example, they would like to be able to employ the pastor full time (to match the number of hours he works in reality) and to offer other urgently needed services such as more trauma counselling. However, they are unable to do this on the current level of income.

As the church looks back, what are some key lessons they have learned which could be of value to others?

A few key lessons are the following:

1. Be flexible and willing to respond to the needs that are actually present, not the needs you assume might be present.
2. Realize that some needs can be better served by other groups and organizations. For example, a lot of groups working in Austria offer immediate aid (blankets, emergency food, bottled water). It would be inefficient to try to duplicate that effort. However, very few groups work with long-term integration.
3. Be aware that even within language groups, the cultural and educational differences between people from different regions can be sharp dividing lines and cause tensions that need to be addressed. For example, while they both speak Farsi, the difference between a university-educated Iranian from Tehran and an illiterate refugee from Afghanistan is enormous, and it needs to be carefully

considered when thinking about questions of indigenous leadership, integration, group dynamics, etc.

4. Take time to hear people's stories. A lot of people who end up as refugees bring compelling stories of trauma and loss with them. It's important to hear these stories and realize what is bubbling below the surface.
5. Stay relationship based. One of the most frequent comments goes along the following lines: "When I left my home country, I lost all my friends and family. And now in this church, I have discovered a new family." Again, this is a dynamic the church can provide that state actors and non-profits generally cannot.
6. Sometimes responding to need means having to pivot strategy *very* quickly. For example, protesting the deportation of an at-risk refugee in their congregation meant the church had to create a peaceful vigil and accompanying media and legal strategy in a matter of hours.
7. Cover everything in prayer. When the kingdom is expanding and people are giving their lives to Christ, it is important to cover everything in prayer to stand against the destructive work of the enemy.

Tempelhof, Berlin, Germany: Ministering to Migrants and Refugees[8]

This church in Berlin has a long history. Their location is in a part of Berlin that has a growing migrant population, and in the summer 2015, they were confronted with an influx of refugees. At this time about forty members of the church came together with the pastor for a brainstorming session where they discussed the question, "How should we as a church react to the visible needs of the displaced?" After this ninety-minute meeting, they had a clear consensus that they must do something.

How did the church start helping refugees?

After deciding to launch a response, the church worked on specific plans on how they could reach out to the refugees in their vicinity. They asked themselves, "What is the physical and emotional condition of these people after their strenuous journey? What is their cultural background? How are

8. We are grateful to Thomas Klammt for providing this case study.

they doing at the refugee camps and homes? How can we make contact with them – would they be willing to receive us?"

It was clear to the church the vast majority of refugees were of a different religion than the church. They decided not to make evangelism or conversion their first priority and instead focused on addressing the refugees' basic needs. They wanted to support the refugees with their everyday burdens while providing them places and times to rest. The church wanted the refugees to be their guests and relax, to experience a positive atmosphere.

What kind of programs and services for refugees does the church have now? How are these programs supported and staffed?

Considering the needs of their guests and the potential of their church, the church decided to offer a German language course and a clothes distribution centre. Two refugee centres were opened very close to the church, and they first reached out there. They approached the managers of the centres and received permission to present invitations to the refugees by placing posters in the Arabic and Farsi languages. They also contacted the huge refugee centre at the Tempelhof Airport buildings, where several thousand refugees were accommodated.

A team of volunteers have been offering a language course for refugees every week since October 2015. They work in small groups and are well accepted by the guests. From here they have also developed private contacts, and several from the course have visited church services.

Also in October 2015, the church opened the clothes distribution centre. Here they collect used clothes from members and offer them to the guests. They also offer coffee and tea, biscuits, and a place to sit and relax. The refugees fill their bag with clothes and then meet with church members for coffee or a time to talk with each other or with one of the volunteers. Sometimes these contacts continue during the week. In this context the members have met an Arabic-speaking pastor, his family, and some other Arab Christians. They now have an Arabic Bible study once a week at the church.

People from at least five different language groups have shown interest in the Christian faith. The church has started Bible study groups in those languages and tries to offer translation of their Sunday worship in three languages (with the help of "churchvox" technology).

The financial expenses are not very high, so for now they can be covered by donations from members. The church had to buy material for the language courses and have to cover the expenses for coffee and biscuits.

The organizational part is more demanding, and the church has to continually ask for donations for the clothes centre. Men's clothes and suitcases are most needed (as there are often no wardrobes in the refugee homes). The volunteer work has to be well organized, and the clothes have to be sorted out and presented well. All work is done for free by volunteers from the church and community.

As the church looks back, what are some key lessons they have learned which could be of value to others?

From the beginning the church's focus was on helping the refugees and showing them a welcoming spirit. This has also changed the church's own people – they started to communicate much more with each other as they worked to fulfil a common task. Many have offered their help or volunteered their time or specific donations. The ministry for their foreign guests has definitely brought positive change to their church.

At their church services, the guests are well visible. They join worship services and other meetings, eat with church members, and also hold their own meetings in the church's facilities. And the church members find that it is not only "us helping them," but they also enrich members through their presence. It is good for members to have these joyful people among them. It is good for members to share their wealth. The guests bring new life into old walls. The members are grateful.

As has been mentioned, the church has an Arabic-speaking group meeting in the church, and a Korean missionary who previously lived in an Arab country has partnered with the church to minister to refugees in Berlin. He had heard of the ministry and wants to support it. Just like him, many others are coming and joining.

The church has experienced God's guidance in many ways and received the support of other Christians they had not previously known. God has sent people at the right time to support the work; otherwise they would not have made it.

The key lesson is this: When a church starts a ministry to the poor, the members have to know that change is going to happen. The church itself will change, and a lot of change will come from outside. When a congregation is ready for this and not afraid, this church recommends ministry among refugees.

Bekaa Valley, Lebanon: Responding to Syrian Refugees[9]

The church is in the Bekaa Valley of Lebanon in the town of Zahle, just a few kilometres from the Syrian border. The town has witnessed many battles between Lebanese militias and the Syrian military during the fifteen-year civil war in Lebanon (1975–1990). The church which started as a home group grew into a congregation of sixty adults.

As Syrian refugees began to flood into Lebanon in 2011, many of the over 1.2 million Syrian refugees settled in informal settlements or in any kind of shelter available in the Bekaa Valley. The Syrian refugees proved to be a challenge, not just because of the large numbers who came, but also because of the prior Syrian occupation of Lebanon. Most Lebanese families have stories of experiencing atrocities committed by the Syrian military during the occupation.

The church's work among the Syrian refugees started with God working in the heart of the pastor, and he was convicted to forgive the Syrians for what they had done to his family during the war. His example encouraged others in the church to move beyond their negative feelings towards Syrian refugees. With assistance from the Lebanese Society for Educational and Social Development (LSESD – also known as the Lebanese Baptist Association), the church started providing food aid packages to a hundred refugee families. This number has since grown, and they now provide assistance to over a thousand families. They also have a school for three hundred refugee children, informal schools in two other locations for another two hundred and fifty children, and income generation projects for refugees. Partnerships with other agencies and groups have provided medical services to the refugees who would otherwise not be able to access medical help.

The church is very aware that it is not a social service agency but a church; all the activities of helping the refugees are considered a part of their witness to Christ and his kingdom. They are very clear about their identity as a Christian Evangelical church. But their help does not come with conditions, and refugees are not required to take any spiritual books or attend any meetings or church services. However, Christian material is available, and refugees are invited to church services and meetings. As a result, many attend the meetings and take the Christian material, and more are starting to attend the church services. The church also holds Discovery Bible Study groups in many of the informal

9. This case study is drawn from the unpublished PhD thesis of Elie Haddad, the president of the Arab Baptist Theological Seminary (ABTS) in Beirut, Lebanon.

settlements of the refugees, to which many others attend. The help provided is on the basis of need, regardless of religion or ethnicity.

Challenges for the church

The traditional teaching in the Lebanese Baptist churches is that the church focus only on spiritual issues. Social and humanitarian work is the responsibility of humanitarian agencies. However, the pastor of this church has a broader understanding of what ministry entails. The majority of members had come to faith and grown spiritually at the church in Zahle. There were not many transfer members. As a result, they grew up with the teaching that ministry involves meeting both the spiritual and physical needs of people.

The church was not prepared for this type of ministry, and the growth of the ministry took them by surprise. They did not have the required people, the expertise, the experience, nor the facilities. The church responded by empowering people to make decisions and by giving them specific responsibilities. The ministry flourished because of this delegation of responsibilities. Many leaders have since emerged, including many Syrian refugees who have come to faith and have become members of the church.

The church experienced a lot of resistance from neighbours because of the traffic congestion and crowds during the food distributions. Because it is a Christian neighbourhood, they were also uncomfortable with Muslim men and women congregating there, with their different ways of dressing. The neighbours were also concerned about potential security threats. They protested regularly and filed complaints with the municipality accusing the church of exacerbating religious tensions.

The church responded positively to the concerns of their Lebanese neighbours. They organized their food distributions and other activities so that they would not cause problems for those living around the church. They started helping the Lebanese poor as well in order to diffuse the resentment that only the Syrians were receiving assistance. Over time, the neighbours began to appreciate the work of compassion that the church was doing.

There were no conditions for the assistance provided. But in spite of the fact that the refugees were not required to attend any meeting or church service, large numbers started attending the Sunday services. Due to the limited space available in the church, they decided to start a second service. This service was more evangelistic in nature and was geared to those from other faiths who were not familiar with Christian vocabulary and forms of worship. Those who had already become followers of Christ would attend the first service where there was more biblical teaching about the Christian faith and life.

Impact of the church's responses to those in need

The results of the church being inclusive and showing compassion to those in desperate need was quite unexpected. Besides nominal Christians growing in their faith in Christ, the number of Muslims who turned up in church wanting to know about Christ and then coming to faith and being baptized was unprecedented. It had always been assumed that the local church would never be effective in reaching Muslims with the gospel. The church members were also impacted as many became involved in serving in these ministries of compassion. There was a sense of renewal within the congregation.

A number of discipleship groups using the Discovery Bible Study material have been formed. Some focus on evangelism and reaching out to their neighbours, while others are used to train new leaders.

One interesting result is that the various Syrian communities began to bond together. Syria is a deeply divided society along religious, ethnic, and political lines. These divisions were evident even in the refugee communities. However, the church would not allow political discussions. The refugees quickly learned that the church operates by different values, and these values started to shape their own attitudes and behaviour. As a result, the Syrians started to act as a unified group regardless of their backgrounds and differences.

The members of the church learned how to be tolerant towards Muslims and their traditions. They learned to appreciate the different faith journeys that Muslims take as they grow in their faith and came to accept certain cultural practices like wearing the hijab and fasting in Ramadan.

Croatia: Responding to Refugees in Transit and in the Neighbouring Country

A small Protestant denomination of forty-eight churches and around two thousand members in Croatia decided to respond to the flood of refugees transiting through Croatia on their way to Western Europe. The government had set up a refugee transit camp initially at Opatovac (on the road from Vukovar to Ilok). The general secretary of the denomination was involved right from the beginning in coordinating with the mayor of Zagreb and other institutions, religious communities, and NGOs to issue a joint appeal to the citizens of their country to help. The churches of the denomination in Zagreb organized themselves to collect and distribute donations locally. They were provided with a space of eighty square meters where they could collect, pack, and distribute the supplies free of charge by a Syrian gentleman who has been living and working in Zagreb for many years. Supplies were collected from churches as well as through IFES (International Fellowship of Evangelical Students) Croatia. Some items which were lacking were purchased locally. The group also received supplies from other local organizations and from organizations in Portugal, the UK, and Sweden. The supplies are shipped from Zagreb to Opatovac. Funding has been provided by local churches and church partners in the US and Sweden.

The church was invited by the Red Cross and the assistant minister of internal affairs to provide assistance inside the camp in Opatovac. They are one of the few organizations that are allowed inside the camp. They partner with some other NGOs to assist them. In addition to volunteers from their own churches, they also have volunteers from other churches and denominations, some citizens from Osijek, and a volunteer from an NGO in Split. They even had a clown to entertain the children with songs and games.

Initially food was provided by the denomination to one thousand individuals. Though the numbers fluctuated, there were on average at least seven thousand in the camp in Opatovac. Later a second camp was opened at Slavonski Brod. The trains transporting refugees arrived between 1:00 and 3:00 am, and the volunteers working in those late hours needed a hot meal. Recognizing the need, the denomination took over the responsibility of feeding one hundred and fifty volunteers during the night shift.

When the route for the refugees through the Balkans was blocked by various countries, the church received notification from the Croatian ministry of internal affairs that the camp in Slavonski Brod would be closing and that the refugees who were in the camp would be moved to Porin, a hotel on the periphery of Zagreb. That hotel became the new asylum centre where efforts would be made to integrate those seeking asylum into Croatian society.

The government expressed an interest in cooperation and extended its gratitude to all organizations working in this refugee crisis, the largest in Europe since WWII. In Porin, the denomination is working hard on integrating refugees into society through humanitarian work and different projects. The local churches are giving lessons in Croatian language and culture on a daily basis. Many of the refugees expressed a desire to take part in regular worship services in those churches. The Lord is providing many opportunities and ways for the refugees to be a part of those services and be in the fellowship with believers around agape meals.

One of the new church projects in Croatia is setting up a safe house for children under the age of eighteen where they can be cared for. The largest need at this point is finding a house in Zagreb that will serve this purpose.

Since the closing of the borders on the Balkan route, the denomination's activities have spread internationally. After Macedonia closed its borders, they started working in Idomeni, Greece. Their humanitarian aid in Greece has been focused on the northern part of the country, which has more than thirteen refugee camps, where they are distributing food and hygiene supplies and building sports playgrounds.

Questions for Reflection and Discussion

1. What struck you or caught your attention as you read the case studies above?
2. What are some questions that came to mind or issues that you felt were not discussed in the case studies above?
3. Are there activities in these case studies that you could do in your context? Are there systems that you could put in place in your ministries?
4. What challenges will you face in your church or context if you decide to respond to the needs of refugees in the community? How would you deal with these challenges?

Responding to the Needs of Sponsored Refugees

Canada has been sponsoring Syrian refugee families to be resettled in their country, in addition to the refugees Canada accepts from across the world through UN resettlement initiatives. There are a number of different refugee sponsorship programs. The Syrian refugee resettlement program is a partnership between the government, churches, and civil society organizations. Churches can also sponsor refugees independently while still enabling the refugees to access the benefits provided by the government. Many churches across Canada are a part of these programs. They participate as either individual churches or as a small group of churches coming together to not only raise the funds but to also provide all that the refugees need to be resettled. Below are the experiences of two churches in different parts of Canada.

An important note; once the refugees arrive in Canada they cease to be refugees but become newcomers. They can be referred to as "refugee-background newcomers" to distinguish them from newcomers who are immigrants.

Dauphin, Manitoba, Canada: Refugee Sponsorship[10]

How did the church start helping refugees?

The church has been an active part of its small Manitoba city (pop. 8,500) for more than a century. This group of roughly one hundred people continues to faithfully seek ways to encourage each other while worshiping God in word and deed. Commitment to helpfulness is part of the congregation's history. Stories of involvement with the Vietnamese boat people in the 1980s pop up in conversations with the older members. Though the refugees did not stay in Dauphin, the church remembers being a friendly and helpful point of entry into Canadian life.

In 2011 the current pastor travelled to Lebanon and witnessed the beginning of the mass Syrian displacement and refugee situation. Through her connections with Canadian Baptist Ministries, she was able to report the stories of how God was working in the darkness of war to bring people to himself. These stories, combined with the positive refugee memory, solidified a willing response to the present need. When the time came to sign up to help, the church was ready and eager and voted overwhelmingly in favour of this venture. Joining with two other Dauphin churches, DIRT (Dauphin Interchurch Refugee Team[11]) was formed, and working with three separate SAHs (Sponsorship Agreement Holders), they determined to sponsor three Syrian refugee families.

Finances flowed in quickly due to the media frenzy, federal election promises to speed up the refugee process, and the generosity of denominational partners. Only months prior to the churches' involvement, the sponsorship process seemed quite clear. They were to fill out forms, pick a family, and get to know them a bit. Then the family was to say yes, the churches were to say yes, and all were to wait upwards of a year for the family's arrival. What transpired was nothing so ordered. In January the churches filed their application, got a

10. We are grateful to Loralyn Lind for providing this case study.

11. DIRT was comprised of two or three members from each of the three church refugee teams. They happened to include a doctor, a lawyer, a retired school principal, a retired police sergeant, and a pastor.

list, picked some numbers, and called the SAHs, and within a few weeks they received a seventy-two-hour notice that the sponsored families were coming. The committee members arrived at the Winnipeg airport to pick up the first of three families on 11 February with a sense of sheer panic; they had no idea what they were doing.

As the church looks back, what are some key lessons they have learned which could be of value to others?

Five months in, the churches are in awe of how God orchestrated this adventure for their new Syrian friends, for their churches, and for the city of Dauphin. A few things stand out as vital to the success so far.

First, none of the participants can imagine this process without the translators DIRT was able to hire. From that first meeting at the airport (and subsequent three-hour journey by van at minus 28 degrees Celsius across the barren Manitoba winter wastelands) to the first meals together in a family home (because their house wasn't ready), having someone to explain and understand meant everything. The group hired a Syrian man for the first three months to serve the three families and shared his costs between the three churches.

The second lesson was the importance of English classes. The first family started government-funded English classes within two days of arriving and have continued with three classes a week since. DIRT agree with the government's insistence on making the acquisition of the official language a priority for the first year. They could see this as a solid gift to give their families as they attempted to settle in their new country. The school-aged child started school the day after he arrived, and he says his school is "seven billion million times" better than the one he attended in Jordan. The churches have struggled a bit getting regular English tutors in the summer, but trust the driving lessons for the men and the tutors for the families will start again in September.

The mountains of paperwork were filled out and signed. The rental houses were moved into, bank accounts procured, bill payment methods figured out, and the computer, TV, and internet were hooked up. All have had medical and dental appointments (inoculations up to date), and the children are now used to car seats (which was not easy). All three families planted gardens and are excitedly enjoying the yields. The three dads are employed (only part time, as they also see the importance of learning English while they have help with funding).

The third lesson is the importance of friends. After the first translator finished his three months, the churches were blessed to find a Syrian woman who had came to Canada in January as a refugee. She graciously came to help them in Dauphin and is about to finish her two months. Having her has meant a new level of communication with the women was possible. Having the first translator was wonderful, but the combination of two different translation angles has been significant in the churches relationships with the families. There is a true family feeling now having enjoyed Ramadan meals together and the celebration of Eid.

One small effort on the part of the DIRT team has possibly had one of the biggest impacts. Their second translator offered to teach them Arabic, so a few of them attempted a couple of classes a week. Their pathetic struggles gave them a clear sense of empathy for their Syrian friends as they have committed to learning a new language. This empathy has helped the team continue to cheer the refugees on in their efforts.

Dauphin, Manitoba, is not very "multicultural," nor is it entirely open to newcomers. That all three families are Muslim was a big concern as the nearest mosque is two hours away. The churches were nervous about the refugees' customs and what they would eat. Should they shake hands? Would people be kind on the street? Other than language, this nervousness continues to be the greatest hindrance to the Syrian families being included in the community. As church people meet and spend time with the Syrian families, they realize that these are delightful, friendly people, and the nervousness dissipates on both sides. The challenge now seems to be helping more people make the effort to invest time.

As the team considers the next six months, they hope to establish a weekly meal with the families to practice English and provide a place for others to get to know them in a friendly atmosphere. This is one of many ideas that they hope will help in the "friend" area. They are continuing to pray that they can be a blessing to their new friends and are actively investigating sponsoring some of their relatives. God is kind and good. And the DIRT team is so thankful for his leading.

Moncton, New Brunswick, Canada: Refugee Sponsorship[12]

How did the church start helping refugees?

Approximately seven years ago, towards the end of a church-sponsored baby shower (for a recently joined African congregant), a long-time member of the

12. We are grateful to Paul Carline for providing this case study.

social action committee noticed a gentleman who was waiting for his wife. After chatting awhile, she asked him, also a recent immigrant, if he had found a home church in Moncton. He and his family would be welcome at this church, she said. He told her that he had little need of God, as his daughter and her family had been refused immigration to Canada. They had to be left behind in the Democratic Republic of Congo (DCR) during the severe conflict and were currently caught in very unfortunate and dangerous circumstances. This led the man to question a just God. This story was taken to the pastor, who in turn approached the deacon's board, who agreed with the church to act as co-sponsors for this family.

Over the subsequent seven years, little was heard from the family until late summer of 2015. Apparently the immigration papers, which had not been approved due to numerous unusual circumstances, had finally come through. Would the church still be willing to act as co-sponsors for this family? After meetings with the pastor, the board of deacons, and others, the decision was made to move forward, as it was important to keep their earlier commitment.

In mid-October the church heard that their sponsored family would be arriving in the early weeks of December. Several church members met to begin to prepare for the arrival of their sponsored family. Seven committees were established with wonderful participation from many church members. They were able to fundraise; source food, clothing, household, and kitchen necessities; and begin reconstruction of a basement apartment. Within approximately six weeks, they were ready for the family to arrive (even if work in the basement apartment wasn't quite completed).

On the day of arrival, members of the welcoming team and a few members from the congregation went to the airport with the father, mother, and brother and some of their African friends to greet and meet the family of five arriving from the Democratic Republic of Congo. It was an emotional and heartwarming reunion for the family who had been separated for so many long years. Tears of joy were in evidence! Only through God's hands could this type of cooperation and preparation have been accomplished.

What kind of programs and services for refugees does the church have now? How are these programs supported and staffed?

Currently the church's co-sponsored family from the DCR has been in Moncton for seven months. Initially the seven teams (construction, clothing, food and supplies, furniture, fundraising, welcoming, and communication) organized to prepare for the family's arrival and were very busy for the six weeks prior.

But they had little information on the "how tos," and with an early change in leadership, they were "flying by the seat of our pants!"

The church's situation at first was different. Their commitment to become a co-sponsor had been made long before the Syrian refugee crisis began to affect public sympathy. Unfortunately due to the ongoing conflict in the DRC, the immigration process for this family was stalled for seven years. As the family is not Syrian, and due to the fact that they came ahead of the current influx of Syrian refugees, the church found it much more difficult to access support and information. Their very able team leader for November and December researched both federal and provincial government websites for information regarding appropriate financial assistance. When their pastor connected them with the Convention of Atlantic Baptist Churches (CABC), they found that the "Guidelines for Refugee Assistance" they had put in place concurred with those of the Convention. The print literature that came after their sponsored family's arrival would have been much more helpful before their arrival.

Interestingly too, because the family was not from Syria (even though they were fleeing terrible conflict), their resettlement was not seen as a newsworthy item. From a PR point of view, the church found that their story did not garner public support financially nor public interest in the way Syrian refugee families have.

MAGMA (Multicultural Association of the Greater Moncton Area) was very helpful in the first weeks with filling forms, arranging orientation/ registration for children's schools, reviewing the responsibilities for co-sponsors, and orientation to the family of their new city, as well as providing initial language training and other services available to immigrant families. As the sponsored family are French speaking, CAFI (the French Multi-Cultural Association equivalent) has been a wonderful resource.

The church's co-sponsor – the sponsored family's father and grandfather and his wife – were also responsible for much of the family's orientation. The First Baptist Sponsorship Ministry construction team continued to upgrade their newly purchased home for the needs of a blended family, and in the early weeks of arrival provided a communication and friendship bridge to the family.

While the initial set-up teams have disbanded, several members of the congregation have continued in a part-time volunteer basis to support the family. They provide a monthly cheque for the family (based on government and CABC suggested guidelines for the first year of residence) on the fifteenth of each month. This is arranged through the church treasurer, and the family pick it up from the church secretary.

The construction team members, who spent so much time at the home when the family arrived, were all invited by the father to a lovely African family dinner at their home. It truly was an indication of the appreciation they have for all the incredible work that was done. The construction team leader along with his wife continues to see the family. He is currently helping to translate immigration forms from a pro bono lawyer (whom the recently formed new immigration committee contacted) for an adopted daughter (now sixteen) who was not allowed to immigrate with the family in December. This situation continues to be a tremendous worry and heartache for the sponsored family. Hopefully the church will be able to make some progress throughout the fall so she can join her family in Moncton.

The FBSM leader for 2016 has been responsible for arranging communication between the church, family, and CABC; for family's mental and dental requests and clothing needs, for ongoing support, and for other issues that may arise. So many other team members have been helpful in meeting needs along the way.

Currently the father of the sponsored family has been taking ESL training at McKenzie College through a private gift. The church found that he was not progressing well at MAGMA due to their course structure, and that the lack of English training was holding him back from job applications in Moncton. Of course for any new immigrant, finding a job that will enable them to support their family is of major importance. Hopefully with language improvement, he will be able to apply for a job in the near future with an hourly rate that meets their needs. Interestingly the three children (two boys and a girl, ages fifteen, thirteen, and nine) are doing well in English skills, as is often the case with immigrant children.

The church membership, staff, and pastor and his wife have been very supportive of this ministry. As they continue on in sponsorship, they see their biggest challenges as being (a) Financial, continuing to meet their financial commitment to the sponsorship ministry (especially through the summer months). (b) Communication. Their sponsored family are French speaking, and the congregation is primarily English speakers. And (c) Religion. The family are affiliated with a Jehovah Witness Church in the area. They may not be comfortable at the church, which makes a sense of affinity with the greater church membership challenging.

As the church looks back, what are some key lessons they have learned which could be of value to others?

The church's sponsorship ministry was put together in a very short timeline – approximately six weeks. Any effort requiring this much work, especially in the weeks preceding Christmas, could have been helped by having a longer timeline. At the same time, they wonder if too much time would have caused interest to fall off or the sense of urgency to fade to the sideline somehow. They remain amazed at how God works through his church to make efforts like this sponsorship ministry work. Such an important reminder: We can never underestimate his power.

Having pertinent information about governmental immigration policy and the CABC guidelines prior to the family's arrival would have been more appropriate. Churches receiving sponsored families are now much better equipped with information on the how tos with checklists, Facebook information, etc.

Questions for Reflection and Discussion

1. What are the key issues that need to be discussed by a local church before they decide to sponsor a refugee family?
2. What services and assistance are available from the government (federal, provincial/state, and local/municipal) that the church can access?
3. Are there other community organizations, churches, or groups that the church could partner with in sponsoring and helping refugee families?
4. What do you think are the basic needs of a refugee family when they arrive in a new country for resettlement?

Guidelines for Churches Wanting to Help Refugees

A number of very good resources provide detailed information on how to help refugees. Depending on the kind of assistance the church is looking to provide, some of the manuals listed below could be of assistance.

- **Refugee Protection Manual**
  http://www.refworld.org/protectionmanual.html

- **Handbook to Determine Refugee Status**
  http://www.refworld.org/docid/4f33c8d92.html
- **Mental Health of Refugees**
  http://apps.who.int/disasters/repo/8699.pdf
- **Resource Guide for Refugee Claimants**
  http://svdptoronto.org/wp/wp-content/uploads/2013/01/Manual-for-Refugees.pdf
- **Refugee Law Reader**
  http://www.refugeelawreader.org/en/
- **The Sphere Standards for Providing Humanitarian Assistance to People Affected by Disasters**
  http://www.ifrc.org/PageFiles/95530/The-Sphere-Project-Handbook-20111.pdf
- **Establishing Legal Services for Immigrant Children**
  http://www.immigrantjustice.org/UICBestPractices

The process of ministering to refugees will vary from country to country depending on who the refugees are, the assistance available to them from the government and other agencies, and the capacity of the church. However, here are some guidelines for when a church is considering becoming involved with refugees.

1. The leadership and the congregation have to decide together to become involved in helping refugees. This type of ministry is not for just a few individuals but needs the involvement of many. Besides making the decision to become involved, the pastor or the pastoral team may want to teach on the biblical basis for such ministries, that God is concerned for the poor, the vulnerable, and the foreigner. Besides being compassionate and helping desperate families in need, the objective is also to reveal the kingdom of God and the God you worship.
2. Identify who else in the community is providing services to refugees and what those services are. Can you partner with them, or are they already stretched in the work they are doing? What services and help for refugees are not available in the community?
3. What government services and assistance are available for the refugees and for those helping the refugees? Is funding available

from the government and/or other organizations for the programs you are planning? What is the scope of the funding – what does it cover and what does it not cover?

4. What are the processes and guidelines you have to adhere to in order to help the refugees?
5. After reviewing all the information you have gathered so far, decide on how you would like to help the refugees. Determine the budget you need to raise from within the church and what you can access from other sources. Identify and recruit people from the congregation who are willing to help and can provide specific skills that are needed. Organize the people for the various tasks – ensure proper leadership and accountability so that nothing is left undone or done improperly. Will you be partnering with organizations and other churches? What will that partnership look like? Make sure that all the details, responsibilities, and expectations are discussed, agreed upon, and written down.
6. Become aware of language and cultural issues related to the refugees. How will you prepare yourself to overcome these barriers? For example, do you know what is acceptable behaviour (like shaking hands and hugging) when relating to members of the opposite sex? If refugees will be coming to your church for activities, how will you communicate values and acceptable behaviour, especially with regards to relationships? How will you deal with cultural problems when they arise?
7. What activities can you do with the refugees that will help them integrate into the local community?
8. How can you help the refugees not only access *space* (a place to live), but also create a new *place* to restart their lives, a place they can make their home? How can you as a community help the refugees develop a new identity – one which incorporates the identity they lost when they left their home country – into the identity of being part of their new country? Are there community and national events you can take them to and explain the significance of to them? Are they aware of the history of the community and the country so that they know where and how they fit? Are there family events you can help them celebrate using symbols from both cultures?

9. As a church community, how will you show the refugees the love of Christ in ways they can understand? How can you help them experience what the kingdom of God is like and introduce them to the king? Remember, conversion is something God does in his way and in his time. Any help you provide should be unconditional and not dependent on the refugees attending church activities. At the same time, we should not be ashamed of who we are and the God we worship. We are asked to be ambassadors of the living God and witness to his reality and love.

Ministering to the Stateless

Very few churches, if any, are involved in ministering intentionally to the stateless largely because of the challenges of the legal issues involved. However, there are examples of faith-based organizations who prioritize the stateless in their services.

Beirut, Lebanon: Responding to the Needs of Stateless Children

Kids Alive Lebanon (KAL)[13] has been serving at-risk children and orphans in the outskirts of Beirut since 1948. Initially founded to meet the massive needs of Palestinian refugee children that emerged during the twentieth century, the organization now provides residential, educational, and care centre services to children of diverse backgrounds. The ministry community includes Lebanese nationals, but the majority of children come from the growing refugee and migrant population. As a Christian faith-based community of teachers and caregivers, they honour the intrinsic value of each child regardless of ethnicity, religion, or legal status. This care is especially extended to children suffering statelessness.

Lebanon has a stateless population numbering between 80,000 and 200,000 people[14] (not including an estimated 450,000 stateless Palestinian refugees).[15] In aiming to rescue children from vulnerable situations, KAL has long ministered directly to the particular needs of stateless children by creating educational

13. KAL is known locally as Dar El Awlad.

14. Institute on Statelessness and Inclusion, *The World's Stateless* (Oisterwijk, The Netherlands: Wolf Legal Publishers, 2014), 107.

15. United Nations Relief and Works Agency for Palestine Refugees in the Near East, "Where We Work," (1 July 2014), www.unrwa.org/where-we-work/lebanon.

opportunities that would otherwise be unavailable to those children lacking identification papers. KAL likewise provides a community of care and protection to stateless individuals who face the constant risks of detainment and deportation due to their lack of legal status. In response to the Syrian civil war and its massive displacement crisis into neighbouring countries, KAL opened a section of its primary school to accommodate Syrian refugees. Students are accepted even if they do not possess official documentation proving a nationality.

KAL's specific concern for stateless children includes a small literacy program in South Lebanon near the city of Sidon. This program exists within a centre partnership that serves nearby Dom (Gypsy) and Bedouin communities. These communities are throughout Lebanon and suffer widespread poverty and marginalization. They have faced significant levels of statelessness due to a combination of causes, including historical exclusion from the Lebanese national community and the prevalence of unregistered marriages and births. Many children lack legal documents and are therefore prohibited from attending public schools. With private schooling unaffordable, they are left without access to education and are at risk to the vulnerabilities that accompany lifelong illiteracy. The KAL literacy program was established specifically to create a learning program for statelessness children. Although not a formal school, it provides undocumented children with their only opportunity to experience learning in a structured environment.

Stateless children are a special concern for KAL. The legal status (or lack thereof) of new applicants is weighed heavily when evaluating the intake of new children. It is well understood that stateless individuals in Lebanon are particularly marginalized, and the organization strategically aims to make its services available to those affected by statelessness. When possible they assist individuals in their quest to attain a citizenship, a process that is complicated and fraught with social, political, and legal roadblocks. KAL's concern for the stateless was on display in a symbolic way at a recent annual fundraiser event. The ceremony featured a presentation of flags of the dozens of nations represented by the children in its programs. Front and centre was a plain white flag representing the stateless children; during the course of the event it was the only flag to receive any specific mention.

Guidelines for Organizations and Churches Wanting to Minister to the Stateless

As this book has detailed, the displaced face a particular form of practical and psychological suffering, and the global Christian community of faith has a biblical mandate to help them belong, both within God's kingdom and within the political systems of our world. This mandate is especially urgent in the ongoing crisis of statelessness, which is prevalent across the globe from Asia and Africa all the way to Europe and the Americas. The stateless are denied the legal right of nationality and are effectively excluded from the international community of nation-states. This problem has widespread impact. However, some resources are available for those wanting to engage statelessness.

- **Learning About Statelessness**
  http://www.statelessness.eu/blog/new-efficient-way-learning-about-statelessness
- **Handbook for Protection of Stateless People (UNHCR)**
  http://www.unhcr.org/protection/statelessness/53b698ab9/handbook-protection-stateless-persons.html
- **Determination Guide on Statelessness**
  http://www.statelessness.eu/sites/www.statelessness.eu/files/attachments/resources/Statelessness%20determination%20and%20the%20protection%20status%20of%20stateless%20persons%20ENG.pdf
- **Handbook on Nationality and Statelessness** (Though it is for parliamentarians, it has valuable information.)
  http://www.ipu.org/PDF/publications/statelessness_en.pdf
- **World Council of Churches Assembly Statement, Recommendations and Webinar on Statelessness**
  https://www.oikoumene.org/en/press-centre/news/wcc-strengthens-call-to-end-statelessness
- **World Council of Churches Bible Study on Statelessness**
  https://www.oikoumene.org/en/resources/documents/bible-study-on-statelessness

Despite its complicated dimensions, statelessness presents many opportunities to show active compassion in the face of a severe injustice, and in doing so reveals the reality of God's kingdom. The following are three pillars on which a church can build a compassionate response to statelessness.

1. **Elevate the awareness of statelessness as a global crisis.** The hardship of being stateless persists in large part because this suffering tragically remains unnoticed by an unaware and uninformed public. Although statelessness is slowly emerging as a focus issue in the fields of human rights advocacy and academic scholarship, it remains widely unaddressed by and within the Christian community.[16] The church is consequently missing opportunities to continue its legacies of facing social ills by advancing causes of justice and human wholeness. Statelessness, with its complex global and local nuances, needs to be properly understood by the greater population.

   One starting point in gaining knowledge about statelessness is the Institute of Statelessness and Inclusion, a Netherlands-based institute dedicated to facilitating research, advocacy, and awareness of statelessness.[17] A wealth of resources and educational opportunities are available through the institute. Additionally, in 2014 the UNHCR launched the #IBELONG campaign, which aims to end statelessness in ten years.[18] The campaign offers current information on the scope and scale of statelessness, a ten-point action plan to directly address the problem, and an open letter to voice popular support. Simply acquiring information about statelessness as a human rights injustice will help direct prayerful and practical responses.

   Many churches are already engaged in development, relief, and mission activities at both local and international levels, and statelessness may be a pressing issue facing people in these ministry contexts. Faith communities and organizations would do well to evaluate the places and the people they serve and research if statelessness is a threat. The painful reality is that statelessness is likely much more prevalent and near than many realize. Before we

16. A major exception to this is the World Council of Churches (WCC), which has specifically highlighted statelessness in recent years by issuing position statements, conducting trainings, and developing Bible devotions centered on the global crisis. These can be accessed on the WCC website. "WCC Strengthens Call to End Statelessness" (2016), https://www.oikoumene.org/en/press-centre/news/wcc-strengthens-call-to-end-statelessness.

17. Institute on Statelessness and Inclusion, "Understanding Statelessness in the Syria Refugee Context" (2016), http://www.institutesi.org/ourwork/displacement.php.

18. UNHCR, "#IBELONG" (2016), http://www.unhcr.org/ibelong/.

can do anything we must know something; the church must become aware of statelessness.

2. **Minister to the needs of the stateless.** Stateless individuals face a host of practical challenges. Many of the necessary services, opportunities, and provisions that are readily available to citizens are elusive to the stateless. It is important for churches to act appropriately to help meet the human needs of the stateless and address their vulnerability. These actions can include helping stateless individuals and families pursue formal education, gain employment, secure housing, access financial loans and assistance, and receive medical care.

   One practical way faith communities can address these problems is by taking actions that help prevent statelessness. These can include the crucial measure of assisting in birth registrations, which is particularly urgent in refugee contexts where the practical and legal realities of displacement leave children at heightened risk of becoming stateless due to barriers in registering births and proving the genuine link needed for establishing citizenship. Just as food, economic, housing, education, and health related services are commonly administered to vulnerable communities, so should services related to official documentation and status.

   The predominant need of all stateless individuals is rather straightforward: legal national status. This can be obtained either in the places of residency or in new places. Churches can use their human and financial resources to help provide legal remedies for individual stateless cases or assist in resettlement to places where citizenship is attainable. Until stateless individuals gain their human right of official nationality, they will face unrelenting exclusion and marginalization. Statelessness will cease when formal citizenship is enjoyed by all.

3. **Advocate for the stateless.** Statelessness is in many ways a legal problem, and its solution requires a fundamental reformation of the nation-state laws and practices that allow it to perpetuate. The Christian community is in a position to advocate for policies that will seriously minimize, even eliminate, the prevalence of statelessness, including advocating for nationality laws that grant women equal rights to men for transmitting citizenship to their children. When

mothers are denied their fundamental right to pass nationality, the door is opened for a host of complications that can lead to childhood statelessness. International human rights demand that women enjoy the same rights as men, and the church's voice is needed to likewise demand that nation-states implement principles of equality in their nationality laws. Additionally, advocacy is needed to see that nation-states meet the international standards on the treatment of stateless populations and the reduction of statelessness. These practices are articulated most authoritatively in the "Convention Relating to the Status of Stateless Persons" of 1954 and the "Convention on the Reduction of Statelessness" of 1961. Statelessness is an absolutely solvable problem, but to solve it requires an active form of advocacy that seeks institutional change in the way nation-states implement policy.

Conclusion

You know, those of us who leave our homes in the morning and expect to find them there when we go back – it's hard for us to understand what the experience of a refugee might be like.

Naomi Shihab Nye, poet, songwriter and novelist[1]

In casually reviewing the popular literature on why Christians should help refugees, the most commonly stated reason is because Jesus was a refugee. While that is a statement of fact, it does not provide the reasons why God is concerned for the well-being of foreigners and strangers who have no family or community to support them. God commanded the ancient Israelites to show compassion to the foreigner, and Jesus repeatedly taught about responding to the needs of the poor, especially those who are strangers who do not belong to our own community. But why is God so concerned for refugees and the displaced?

There are numerous recent books that focus on the details of how to help refugees, whether the refugees are being sponsored or are displaced and desperate for assistance. This book has instead sought to answer the question of whether as Christians we have a responsibility to assist the displaced. We have sought to explore *the biblical, theological, and missiological foundations for any ministry to the displaced.*

We have focused on those who have been forcibly displaced while acknowledging that voluntary migration can be a blessing to the church, to the places where the migrants live, and to the individual migrants themselves. Yet displacement of any kind is deeply destructive to individuals as they are threatened with losing their identity and sense of who they are as a result of being uprooted from their home and all that is familiar. Their marginalization undermines the important sense of personal value and hinders opportunities to be meaningful contributors to the society around them. This destruction of identity and worth is offensive to God; it attacks the image of God in the

1. Naomi Shihab Nye, "Naomi Shihab Nye Quotes," Brainy Quote, https://www.brainyquote.com/quotes/quotes/n/naomishiha530949.html.

person. Timothy Laniak explains that because human beings everywhere bear God's image and likeness, he has a stake in how humans are treated and what happens to them.[2] The distortion of the image of God caused by displacement and the severity of its consequences means that believers must be concerned about the crises facing refugees, migrants, and the stateless, and this concern must lead to an active compassion.

Much humanitarian assistance has focused on meeting the immediate needs of the displaced – needs such as shelter, food, access to health care, re-establishing livelihoods, accessing jobs, and educating children. What has not been understood are the emotional and psychological needs of the displaced and their loss of identity and belonging. While many of the forcibly displaced have experienced horrific traumas from the conflicts they have escaped from, the deeper and longer term trauma is the loss of roots. They become listless and paralyzed because they do not know what to do. They no longer have the skills, the networks, nor the resources to provide for themselves and be contributing members of society. They face the humiliation of being dependent on others; they feel they have been reduced to being beggars. In the process, they lose their culture and traditions which used to help them celebrate the passing of the seasons, enjoy special occasions, and cope with tragedy. They no longer have a place they can call home and are unable to see how life should continue.

So how should communities of faith and the people of God respond?

The key is to recognize refugees, migrants, and the stateless as human beings of worth, value, and meaning. They are not *problems* to be solved but are *persons* who need help. In ministering to the vulnerable and marginalized, we minister to God directly. Jesus, while teaching about the behaviour and attitudes his followers should have, said,

> For I was hungry and you gave me something to eat, I was thirsty and you gave me something to drink, I was a stranger and you invited me in, I needed clothes and you clothed me, I was sick and you looked after me, I was in prison and you came to visit me. . . . "Truly I tell you, whatever you did for one of the least of these brothers and sisters of mine, you did for me." (Matt 25:35–36, 40)

2. Laniak, *Finding the Lost Images*, 48.

Mother Teresa often said that she saw God in those who had been abandoned in spite of their dirt, filth, brokenness, and poverty.[3] She was able to see them as body, soul, and spirit, reflecting the mystery of the Trinity. Like every other human being, they are someone of value whom God had created as the pinnacle of creation. In the person's suffering, one sees what the suffering of Christ would have looked like – Christ who is Creator, the God who is the source of life, who took on human form and experienced the suffering and pain of the world. Mother Teresa then wrote what our response should be.

> We make ourselves live the love of God in prayer and in our work, through a life characterized by the simplicity and humility of the Gospel. We do this by . . . loving and serving [Jesus] hidden under the painful guise of the poorest of the poor, whether their poverty is a material poverty or a spiritual one. We do this by recognizing in them (and giving back to them) the image and likeness of God.[4]

Mary Jo Leddy, a refugee advocate and founder of Romero House in Toronto, Canada, refers to a longitudinal study (the Refugee Resettlement Project) done by Morton Beiser at Ryerson University in Toronto. In that study he had asked refugees, mostly Vietnamese boat people, what had helped them the most to integrate into their new society. Their answer was "warmth of welcome." Mary Jo Leddy writes, "Isn't that interesting? Employment, housing, English classes – those things are important, but it was a personal, caring connection that was the key to successful integration."[5]

This "warmth of welcome" is the hospitality and embrace that Miroslav Volf writes about. It is not just about providing for the physical needs of those who have been displaced. It is about valuing them as human beings. As the displaced experience being valued, they can start making their places into homes and claim a sense of belonging in this world.

---

3. Mother Teresa is supposed to have said every time she pulled a beggar from the gutter that she saw Jesus Christ. "They are Jesus. Everyone is Jesus in a distressing disguise." Suffering.net, http://www.suffering.net/servmo-t.htm.

4. Mother Teresa, *In My Own Words,* compiled by Jose Luis Gonzalez-Balado (Linguori, MO: Linguori Publications, 1996), 108.

5. "A Kolbe Times Interview with Mary Jo Leddy," *Kolbe Times* (11 September 2016), http://www.kolbetimes.com/a-kolbe-times-interview-with-mary-jo-leddy/.

Bibliography

Accad, Martin. "'The World Is Yours!' A Brief Reflection on Citizenship and Stewardship." *The Institute of Middle East Studies* (30 July 2015). https://imeslebanon.wordpress.com/2015/07/30/the-world-is-yours-a-brief-reflection-on-citizenship-and-stewardship/.

Arendt, Hannah. *Origins of Totalitarianism*. Cleveland, OH: World, 1958.

Atkins, Margaret, and Robin Osborne. *Poverty in the Roman World*. Cambridge: Cambridge University Press, 2006. doi:10.1007/s13398-014-0173-7.2.

Barnett, Michael, and Janice Stein. *Sacred Aid: Faith and Humanitarianism*. Oxford: Oxford University Press, 2012. doi:10.1093/acprof:oso/9780199916023.001.0001.

Bartholomew, Craig G. *Where Mortals Dwell: A Christian View of Place for Today*. Grand Rapids, MI: Baker Academic, 2011.

Blitz, Brad K. *Forced Migration Policy Briefing 3: Statelessness, Protection and Equality*. Oxford: Oxford Department of International Development, University of Oxford, 2009.

Boesen, Jacob Kirkeman, and Tomas Martin. *Applying a Rights-Based Approach: An Inspirational Guide For Civil Society*. Copenhagen: Danish Institute for Human Rights, 2007.

Bosch, David J. *A Spirituality of the Road*. Eugene, OR: Wipf & Stock, 1979.

Brown, Peter. *Poverty and Leadership in the Later Roman Empire. The Menahem Stern Jerusalem Lectures*. Hanover, NH: University Press of New England, 2002.

Brueggemann, Walter. "How the Early Church Practiced Charity." *The Christian Century*, June (2003).

———. *The Land: Place as Gift, Promise, and Challenge in Biblical Faith*. 2nd ed. Minneapolis, MN: Augsburg Fortress, 2002.

Burnside, Jonathan. *The Status and Welfare of Immigrants: The Place of the Foreigner in Biblical Law and Its Relevance to Contemporary Society*. Cambridge: Jubilee Centre, 2001.

Das, Rupen. *Compassion and the Mission of God: Revealing the Hidden Kingdom*. Carlisle: Langham Global Library, 2016.

de Vaux, Roland. *Ancient Israel: Its Life and Institutions*. London: Darton, Longman & Todd, 1965.

Edwards, Adrian. "Global Forced Displacement Hits Record High." *UNHCR*, 2016.

Escobar, Samuel. "New Testament Theological Basis." Oxford, 2016.

Farmer, Paul. *Pathologies of Power: Health, Human Rights, And The New War On The Poor*. Berkeley, CA: University of California Press, 2005.

Fensham, Frank C. "Widows, Orphans, and the Poor in Ancient Near Eastern Legal and Wisdom Literature." In *Essential Papers on Israel and the Ancient Near East*, edited by Fredreick E. Greenspan, 176–92. New York, NY: New York University Press, 2000. doi:10.1086/371679.

Ferris, Elizabeth. "Faith-Based and Secular Humanitarian Organizations." *International Review of the Red Cross* 87, no. 858 (2005): 311–25. doi:10.1017/S1816383100181366.

Gellner, Ernest. *Muslim Society*. Cambridge: Cambridge University Press, 1981. doi:10.2307/2801736.

Geneva Convention. "Convention and Protocol Relating to the Status of Refugees." Geneva, 1951.

Glasser, Arthur F., Charles E. Van Engen, Dean S. Gilliland, Shawn B. Redford, and Paul Hiebert. *Announcing the Kingdom: The Story of God's Mission in the Bible*. Grand Rapids, MI: Baker Academic, 2003.

Groody, Daniel G. *Crossing the Divide: Foundations of a Theology of Migration and Refugees*, Monograph 15. Oxford: Crowther Centre Monographs, 2010.

Gutiérrez, Gustavo. "Memory and Prophecy." In *The Option for the Poor in Christian Theology*, edited by Daniel G. Groody, 17–40. Notre Dame, IN: University of Notre Dame Press, 2007.

Harland, Philip A. "The Economy of First-Century Palestine: State of the Scholarly Discussion." In *Handbook of Early Christianity: Social Science Approaches*, edited by Anthony J. Blasi, Jean Duhaime, and Philip-Andre Turcotte, 511–27. Walnut Creek, CA: Alta Mira Press, 2002.

Heather, Peter. "Refugees and the Roman Empire," 2015. https://podcasts.ox.ac.uk/refugees-and-roman-empire.

Institute on Statelessness and Inclusion. *The World's Stateless*. Oisterwijk, The Netherlands: Wolf Legal Publishers, 2014.

———. "Understanding Statelessness in the Syria Refugee Context," 2016. http://www.institutesi.org/ourwork/displacement.php.

Jenkins, Philip. *The Next Christendom: The Coming of Global Christianity*. New York, NY: Oxford University Press, 2007.

Jones, Ben, and Marie Juul Petersen. "Instrumental, Narrow, Normative? Reviewing Recent Work on Religion and Development." *Third World Quarterly* 32, no. 7 (2011): 1291–1306. doi:10.1080/01436597.2011.596747.

Kolbe Times. "A Kolbe Times Interview with Mary Jo Leddy." *Kolbe Times*, 2016. http://www.kolbetimes.com/a-kolbe-times-interview-with-mary-jo-leddy/.

Koyama, Kosuke. "'Extended Hospitality to Strangers': A Missiology of Theologica Crucis." *International Review of Mission* LXXXII, no. 327 (1993): 283–95.

Kraft, Kathryn. "Faith and Impartiality in Humanitarian Response: Lessons from Lebanese Evangelical Churches Providing Food Aid." *International*

Review of the Red Cross 97, no. 897–898 (2015): 395–421. doi:10.1017/S1816383115000570.

Kreider, Alan. *The Patient Ferment of the Early Church: The Improbable Rise of Christianity in the Roman Empire*. Grand Rapids, MI: Baker Academics, 2016.

Laniak, Timothy S. *Finding the Lost Images of God*. Grand Rapids, MI: Zondervan, 2010.

Lohfink, Norbert. "Poverty in the Laws of the Ancient Near East and the Bible." *Theological Studies* 52, no. 1 (1991): 34–50.

Longenecker, Bruce. *Remember the Poor: Paul, Poverty, and the Greco-Roman World*. Grand Rapids, MI: Eerdmans, 2010.

Malina, Bruce J. "Collectivism in Mediterranean Culture." In *Understanding the Social World of the New Testament*, edited by Richard E. DeMaris and Dietmar Neufeld, 17–28. London: Routledge, 2010. doi:10.4324/9780203865149.

McGill, Jenny. *Religious Identity and Cultural Negotiation: Toward a Theology of Christian Identity in Migration*. Eugene, OR: Pickwick, 2016.

Meeks, Wayne A. *The First Urban Christians: The Social World of the Apostle Paul*. New Haven, CT: Yale University Press, 1983.

Moltmann, Jürgen. *The Crucified God*. London: SCM Press, 1974.

OCHA. "Guiding Principles on Internal Displacement." *United Nations*. New York, NY, 1998. doi:10.2307/2547706.

Odinkalu, Chidi Anselm. "Why More Africans Don't Use Human Rights Language." In *Human Rights Dialogue: Human Rights for All? The Problem of the Human Rights Box*. New York, NY: Carnegie Council on Ethics and International Affairs, 2000.

Office of the United Nations High Commissioner for Human Rights. *The Rights of Non-Citizens*. Geneva: United Nations, 2006.

Pleins, J. David. *The Social Visions of the Hebrew Bible: A Theological Introduction*. Louisville, KY: Westminster John Knox Press, 2001.

Shihab, Naomi. "Naomi Shihab Nye," 2009. https://www.brainyquote.com/quotes/quotes/n/naomishiha530949.html.

The International Federation of Red Cross and Red Crescent Societies and the ICRC. "The Code of Conduct for the International Red Cross and Red Crescent Movement and NGOs in Disaster Relief," 1995. http://www.ifrc.org/Docs/idrl/I259EN.pdf.

The UN Refugee Agency. *Global Trends - Forced Displacement in 2015*. Edited by UNHCR. Geneva, 2015.

UN General Assembly. "International Convention on the Protection of the Rights of All Migrant Workers and Members of Their Families (CMW). Resolution 45/158 of 18 December 1990." New York, NY, 1990.

———. "International Convention on the Protection of the Rights of All Migrant Workers and Members of Their Families (CMW). Resolution 45/158 of 18

December 1990," 1990. http://www.ohchr.org/EN/ProfessionalInterest/Pages/CMW.aspx.

UN General Assemby. "Convention on the Reduction of Statelessness," 1961. http://www.ohchr.org/Documents/ProfessionalInterest/statelessness.pdf.

UNHCR. "#IBELONG," 2016. http://www.unhcr.org/ibelong/.

———. "1954 Convention Relating to the Status of Stateless Persons." *UNHCR 60 Years*, 2013. http://www.ohchr.org/Documents/ProfessionalInterest/stateless.pdf.

———. "Conventions and Protocol Relating to the Status of Refugees," 2010. http://www.unhcr.org/protect/PROTECTION/3b66c2aa10.pdf.

———. "Figures at a Glance: Global Trends 2015," 2016. http://www.unhcr.org/en-us/figures-at-a-glance.html.

United Nations. "International Migration and Development," 2016. http://esa.un.org/unmigration/wallchart2016.htm.

———. "The Universal Declaration of Human Rights." *United Nations*. New York, NY, 1948.

United Nations Information Service (UNIS). "Press Release - It Takes Courage to Be a Refugee," 2005. http://www.unis.unvienna.org/unis/pressrels/2005/unisinf84.html.

UNRWA. "Where We Work." Accessed 9 December 2015. www.unrwa.org/where-we-work/lebanon.

Volf, Miroslav. *Exclusion and Embrace: A Theological Exploration of Identity, Otherness, and Reconciliation*. Nashville, TN: Abingdon, 1996.

von Harnack, Adolf. *The Mission and Expansion of Christianity in the First Three Centuries*. Translated. New York, NY: Harper & Brothers, 2005.

Weil, Simone. *The Need for Roots*. New York, NY: G. P. Putnam's Sons, 1952.

Winter, David, Rachel Brown, Stephanie Goins, and Clare Mason. *Trauma, Survival and Resilience in War Zones: The Psychological Impact of War in Sierra Leone and Beyond*. London: Routledge, 2016. doi:10.4324/9781315755922.

Wolterstorff, Nicholas. *Justice: Rights and Wrongs*. Princeton, NJ: Princeton University Press, 2008.

Woodberry, D., and R. Shubin. "Why I Chose Jesus." *Mission Frontiers*, 2001. http://www.missionfrontiers.org/2001/01/muslim.htm.

World Council of Churches. "WCC Strengthens Call to End Statelessness," 2016. https://www.oikoumene.org/en/press-centre/news/wcc-strengthens-call-to-end-statelessness.

Wright, Christopher J. H. "An Old Testament Perspective." Paper presented at the Stott-Bedaiko Forum "The Refugee Crisis: Our Common Human Condition," Oxford University, 2016.

Langham Literature and its imprints are a ministry of Langham Partnership.

Langham Partnership is a global fellowship working in pursuit of the vision God entrusted to its founder John Stott –

> ***to facilitate the growth of the church in maturity and Christ-likeness through raising the standards of biblical preaching and teaching.***

Our vision is to see churches in the majority world equipped for mission and growing to maturity in Christ through the ministry of pastors and leaders who believe, teach and live by the Word of God.

Our mission is to strengthen the ministry of the Word of God through:

- nurturing national movements for biblical preaching
- fostering the creation and distribution of evangelical literature
- enhancing evangelical theological education

especially in countries where churches are under-resourced.

Our ministry

Langham Preaching partners with national leaders to nurture indigenous biblical preaching movements for pastors and lay preachers all around the world. With the support of a team of trainers from many countries, a multi-level programme of seminars provides practical training, and is followed by a programme for training local facilitators. Local preachers' groups and national and regional networks ensure continuity and ongoing development, seeking to build vigorous movements committed to Bible exposition.

Langham Literature provides majority world preachers, scholars and seminary libraries with evangelical books and electronic resources through publishing and distribution, grants and discounts. The programme also fosters the creation of indigenous evangelical books in many languages, through writer's grants, strengthening local evangelical publishing houses, and investment in major regional literature projects, such as one volume Bible commentaries like *The Africa Bible Commentary* and *The South Asia Bible Commentary.*

Langham Scholars provides financial support for evangelical doctoral students from the majority world so that, when they return home, they may train pastors and other Christian leaders with sound, biblical and theological teaching. This programme equips those who equip others. Langham Scholars also works in partnership with majority world seminaries in strengthening evangelical theological education. A growing number of Langham Scholars study in high quality doctoral programmes in the majority world itself. As well as teaching the next generation of pastors, graduated Langham Scholars exercise significant influence through their writing and leadership.

To learn more about Langham Partnership and the work we do visit **langham.org**

CPSIA information can be obtained
at www.ICGtesting.com
Printed in the USA
BVHW071656091219
566104BV00011B/694/P

9 781783 682775